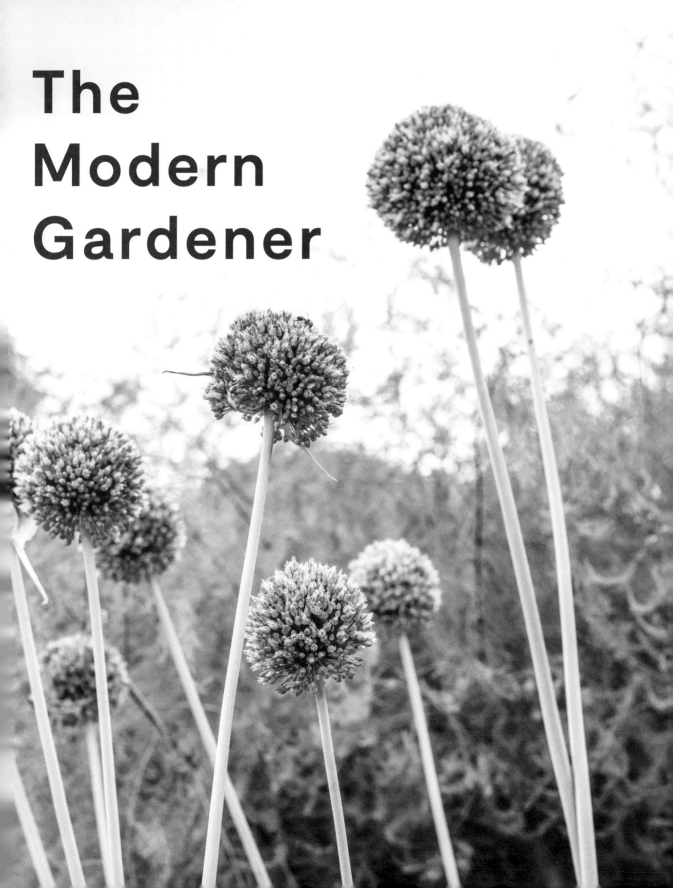

The
Modern
Gardener

Leek 'Poireau perpetuel'

Frances Tophill

A practical guide to gardening creatively, productively and sustainably

The Modern Gardener

Contents

Introduction

The Victorians used to endlessly debate the nature of horticulture. Was gardening an art or a craft or a science? When I first learned about the fervour of these debates I found them faintly ridiculous. Now, however, they seem very relevant. I think, perhaps, it is time we had a debate of our own. And ours should be based on ecology and sustainability. We should be arguing the case for gardens as an essential and untapped part of our ecosystem; a place for productivity and reducing our personal impact on the world's resources.

For too long the default garden has been the square lawn, flanked by lines of plants, bought in non-recyclable, plastic pots, from who knows where and grown using who knows what methods. We have scattered chemicals and expected our gardens to be clinical, clean and neat, free from pests and fallen leaves. But many of us now feel that the outdoors should not be sanitised. I am not 'modern' by any stretch of the imagination; computers overwhelm me; give me a book over a screen any day. I was one of the last people I knew to get a smartphone and I have no idea what the latest fashion trends may be. Modern in the context of this book does not mean visually on-trend. The 'modern' school of thought I want to explore is that our little patches of earth can be a larder, a beauty shop, a wildlife haven, an apothecary, an escape, a connection to nature and to our community; a patch of productive wilderness.

Thousands of years ago cultivating plants started off as a means of guaranteeing food, but later a garden became either a must-have status symbol for kings, queens, courtiers and cardinals – or a purely functional space for growing necessities to eat, brew with and make herbal medicine with. During the Age of Enlightenment across Europe, horticulture became part of the hunger for scientific, engineering and artistic progress. Large nurseries and botanical institutions sent plant hunters across the globe, to wherever respective empires were being built. These intrepid botanists brought plants back home to study, to propagate from and to sell. This is a legacy that is still being unpicked – the ramifications of which, ethically, ecologically and culturally, are being faced up to by botanical institutions and historians, particularly in the western world. Horticulture, however seemingly innocent, can have real-life impacts on the global political landscape. Bioprospecting did and still very much does have a significant contribution to political and economic instability in low and middle-income countries.

We have grown up in a world where if we want something, we buy it. We have taken flora from all over the world without questioning how sustainable or how rare and endangered the plants are in their native habitats or how they are used by indigenous peoples. We have become desensitised to our plants' amazing, diverse appearances and very few of us stop to think where these plants have actually come from or how they were collected.

It is worth saying at this point that my own personal history of gardening has brought me slowly to consider these things. I started without questioning the traditional 'wisdom' and confess to having used chemicals, dug ground, weeded meticulously and mercilessly and bought plants from who knows where in my time. Slowly, though, through meeting amazing people, discussing and practising lower-impact methods and finding inspiration from lots of research. I'm convinced more and more emphatically that there are other ways to garden. Ways that are not only less harmful, but can actively improve the world around us and our own lives with some very simple changes.

The modern gardener

Modern gardeners have a huge desire to reconnect with nature, and to do this in a way that impacts minimally on the planet. Physically, a modern garden can be any size or shape. It can be a pot, a balcony, a little plot or even a shared public space that we work in with other people in the community.

Aesthetically, the 'modern' garden can be anything at all if it suits our tastes, and provides us with a usable and social space, where form is essentially less important than function. As well as being a space in which we can do our bit to provide for the planet and all its creatures, we also want our gardens to provide for us – not just our food, but the materials that feed into the lifestyle choices we make and our hobbies: I have found that making dyes, alcohol, cosmetics, teas and even medicines from the plants that I grow indoors and outdoors has really changed the way I garden and the way I shop, and I would actively encourage everybody to explore the other properties of plants.

As well as enriching our lives, we want our gardens to inspire, educate and tempt our children away from their screens. In short, modern gardeners ask an awful lot from our gardens, and feel the need to use it to give back to nature. We can – and should – expect all of these things from an outdoor space.

The aim of this book

Progress isn't all about money and technology, it's about sensitivity, understanding, resourcefulness and in some ways, restraint. The legacy for this modern generation of gardeners could be a world in which we begin to turn the tide on the 'progress' we have made hitherto. So throughout this book I will look at ways of reducing water and chemical use whilst still managing to keep pests from taking over and at how each of us can make our gardens a haven for wildlife. These small steps to rebalancing the natural world may seem insignificant but eventually they will create vital links through the country and the world to help improve things globally. The book will also be peppered with useful recipes for all kinds of things that I have learnt through my time as a gardener and from some of the wonderful cooks, herbalists and generally lovely people I have been lucky enough to work with.

My aim is to encourage self-reliance, sustainable practices, thinking about further-reaching impacts of the gardening decisions we make, and encouraging everyone to reconnect with some of the processes we have lost. This is about being cutting-edge by stepping back: relaxing, balancing our needs with environmental concerns, and gardening in a time frame that suits us.

Wildlife + Eco-friendly Gardening

1

Wildlife in the garden really matters. It matters for the sake of the wildlife itself, and it also matters for the sake of the garden. A garden that welcomes all creatures can provide a safe haven in a world that is increasingly perilous for native species of insects, mammals, birds, spiders, invertebrates and the whole magical plethora of organisms that exists in the air, the plants and the soil. Creating a space that provides for these species will, in turn, start the processes of building a rich, diverse, self-sustaining and healthy ecosystem within your garden. That includes bacteria and fungi, many of which we will never even know are there, but which are crucially important to our environment, the health of our plants, and even to our own physical health.

At first this can reduce productivity, but once this tapestry begins to build up, you will find that you become more successful as a gardener. There will inevitably be a few pests and nuisances on your plants, but a balanced ecosystem brings natural predators to stop any one pest gaining too much dominance. This will mean that far less intervention is required from you to maintain your garden to a healthy standard, and also that far more pollinators are present to give you bumper crops and flowers.

Being eco-friendly comes into every part of the gardening year, from buying plants to planting, maintaining the garden as well as disposing of waste. The elements of eco-friendly gardening and wildlife-friendly gardening can go hand in hand, maximizing productivity, reducing waste, saving you time and money and making your garden a tangible contributor to improving the environment at large.

Key considerations
for wildlife

Creating environments

Every species requires a different environment. Some like it dark and dusty, others damp; some prefer the safety of the trees and others burrow in the ground. Providing varying, distinct environments within your garden, no matter how small, will be doing a huge service to many endangered and infinitely valuable species.

Breeding sites

Producing and raising offspring is crucial to a species' survival. Providing various suitable breeding sites in your garden will pay dividends – think water, nooks and crannies, trees or shrubs and a place free from pets. Try not to disturb these areas. You can add to any natural features by also providing nesting boxes targeting specific bird, bat and mammal species.

Feeding sites

Once the wildlife is in the garden and breeding, it needs sustenance. The more wildlife you have in the garden, the more competition there will be for the available resources, and the last thing you want is them turning to your crops for food. The best thing you can do is provide varied natural food sources for your wildlife, including plants. When we think of providing food for our wildlife, we tend to go straight to the birdseed, yet this will only provide sustenance for a few species. It's better to create a varied and rich ecosystem filled with seeds, fruits, insects, invertebrates, plant material and everything in between. This will provide abundant food for a huge variety of species. Frogs eat mainly insects and slugs, snakes eat frogs, bats eat night-flying insects, birds eat worms and insects or fruits and seeds, insects eat other insects or decaying plant material and so on.

Drinking and bathing

Water is the backbone of life. A pond, no matter how small, will provide drinking water and bathing for every kind of insect and animal. Many insects and amphibians also rely on water as part of their life cycle, either for breeding or as a nursery for juveniles. For that, a larger body of water will be really helpful, with a deep end of at least 60cm (24in) and a shallow end, preferably with a beach of stones. Be sure to provide a slope of wood or stones so that any accidental swimmers can clamber out again. Fish are a no-no for wildlife ponds, as they tend to feed prolifically, and most insects and amphibians will struggle to drink there, let alone breed or live.

Burrowing and nesting

Nests can be created in a host of places: boxes, trees, buildings, the ground, in plants, in the open and in little nooks and crannies. Providing space for nests but also material with which to make them is really helpful. Most animals are pretty resourceful and can forage nesting material, but reducing their journey time reduces the risks they take and ensures their enterprises are more successful. This is especially important in urban areas, where the larger landscape may simply not offer much in the way of nesting material.

Many animals use leaves, grasses, hay, twigs, chewed-up wood, mud or similar organic materials, while others will just crawl into a welcoming space to set up residence, so providing bat and bird boxes can be helpful. Many species simply burrow into the ground. Insects have various preferences but insect houses are easy to make and a fun project for children. Pile up sticks and leaves, stones and bricks, and drill little holes. It is all useful for different kinds of communal and solitary insects and can also make a striking garden feature.

Plants for wildlife

Plant choice can have a huge impact on the effectiveness of our wildlife gardens – think about choosing plants to provide fruits, seeds, leaves, spikes, pollen, nectar, twigs, nesting material, hiding places, shade and basking places for insects. The list goes on. Remember that specific animals need specific plants, so do your research. Anything with double flowers will not provide pollen, seeds or fruit, so is fairly useless for wildlife.

Spiky branches offer safe nesting sites, big leaves create shade for small mammals and sunbathing for butterflies, while ground-cover plants provide spaces for beetles to hunt and hide. Try to provide flowers: scent, pollen, seeds, fruits, colour, stems and leaves for as much of the year as possible, in as much of the garden as possible! By filling your garden with the greatest variety of plants as you can, you'll attract the widest range of animals, insects, fungi and bacteria.

Left: Cinnabar moth caterpillars feeding on the biennial weed ragwort (*Senecio jacobaea*)

Hawthorn jelly

Hawthorn, or mayflower (*Crataegus monogyna*), is a lovely plant that provides so very much in the garden or in a hedgerow, offering a safe haven and bountiful feast for nesting birds and pollinators. It's also an incredibly useful plant for us. The edible spring leaves are great in salads, and the autumn berries, or haws, can be used in lots of dishes and drinks.

Makes 4 x 450g (1lb) jars

1.3kg (3lb) hawthorn berries

1 teaspoon spices of your choice (ground ginger, nutmeg, cinnamon, allspice)

1 litre (1¾ pints) water

juice of 1 lemon

1.3kg (3lb) sugar

1. Thoroughly wash the berries and remove any stalks.
2. Place the berries and spices in a large pan, cover with the water and simmer on a low heat for 2 hours.
3. Strain through muslin into a clean pan and discard the haws. You can leave it to drip overnight if it's easier.
4. Add the lemon juice and sugar to the strained liquid and place back on the hob over a low heat, stirring until the sugar has dissolved.
5. Increase the heat and bring to the boil. Boil for at least 10 minutes or until it reaches setting point. To test, drip a little of the mixture onto a cold plate. If it wrinkles on the surface when it's tilted or pushed, then it's ready.
6. Pour the jelly into sterilized jars, put the lids on, and store in a cool, dark place until you're ready to eat it.

N.B. Add herbs of your choice for extra medicinal benefits.

Safe passage

Although we want wildlife to stay in our gardens, the reality is that most of us will have visitors that come and go. They will move from their nest or den to breed, feed and drink. Corridors that allow movement around the garden, without running too much of a risk of attack from predators, will allow the wildlife to make successful homes in our plots. These corridors can be little hedges, big hedges, clever layered fences, pergolas covered in climbers or even flower beds. It helps to connect different areas with these corridors, as wide open spaces are inherently dangerous to wildlife.

Entry and exit points

Many species (particularly ground-dwelling ones, like hedgehogs) may struggle to get safely in and out of our gardens but they need to access the wider world, to find food and mates. Be sure to make small holes at the base of your boundaries, or leave small gaps here and there to allow wildlife to come and go freely.

Hibernation

Not all animals and insects hibernate, but for those that do, a warm, cosy and safe space is essential. Hedgehog houses are becoming increasingly popular for this reason. Many solitary bees also hibernate and will benefit from a little tube, like a bamboo cane, in which they can lay their eggs and spend the winter. Be mindful of the species that may be quietly sleeping in our gardens in wood stores, compost heaps or sheds over the winter months and try to cause them minimal disturbance. Checking bonfire piles for hedgehogs is also a very worthwhile enterprise in autumn and winter.

Human and domestic animal disturbance

Dogs, cats, children, hedge trimmers, chainsaws, loud noises, sharp teeth – all of these things are part and parcel of a working family garden. They are not, however, hugely beneficial to healthy, happy, well-rested, long-lived wildlife. If you know that your garden suffers from any or all of these afflictions, and you have the room, I would strongly recommend fencing off an area and leaving it solely to the wildlife. Having a space like this can be a fantastic educational tool for children. Cutting the hedges at the right time of the year (not in the spring or early summer) will mean you are not destroying birds' nests. It is illegal to disturb a bird's nest intentionally, so check before attempting any maintenance on hedgerows, shrubs and trees.

Chemicals

The simple rule is DON'T USE THEM. Destroying even one species with chemicals – whether a plant, fungus or insect – will invariably destroy a whole swathe. There are no species-specific chemical interventions. Poisons work their way up and along the food chain. For example, cats have been known to be poisoned by eating birds who have eaten slugs who have eaten slug pellets. Use instead biological pest controls, such as nematodes and larvae, which can be bought with ease, and target specific species.

Strong fertilizers in the ground can upset the balance of microbial life both above and below the soil. Natural sources of fertilizer like manure and compost are much less harmful. Basically, if you want wildlife, stop using chemicals. And an added bonus is that this will also save you money and time.

Right: Blackfly-infested cardoon, benefiting from a predatory ladybird

Acceptance

Rats, snakes, spiders, wasps, flies, foxes, fungi, bacteria. The list goes on. None of these things fills a gardener with joy — especially if you own any livestock. They are nonetheless a part of the natural world and there isn't really any feasible way of excluding them and welcoming only the things we want. The answer is to embrace these supposedly undesirable characters at least in some parts of the garden and educate ourselves about their vitally important jobs.

Many wasps and flies will pollinate as well as provide a fantastic decomposition service, and spiders and wasps will be effective pest controls. Bacteria facilitate many natural and essential processes, including inside our own bodies, and more and more research is indicating that the fungi in the soil offer channels of communication and help plants with nutrient uptake and even to fight disease through a frugal web that connects their roots. They enable life to exist. So, we need not, and should not, remove them.

Keep other problem species away from the house. Feeding the birds at the far end of the garden will keep any rats away, for instance. Avoid rat poison, which will have a hugely harmful effect on the rest of the wildlife and even your pets, as the poison moves up the food chain. If rats are becoming a problem, provide bird food in other forms such as fruit, or stop feeding the birds until the rats have moved on. Foxes and snakes can be helpful in keeping populations of other species in check.

Key considerations for eco-friendly gardening

Peat vs. peat-free composts

Peat, which has long been used in composts, is a finite resource that is proving very difficult to regenerate. Peat bogs are threatened habitats that provide for many species, including the sphagnum moss that creates the environment itself. Horticultural peat currently makes up 1 per cent of the peat used worldwide; the vast majority is used for fuel. However, horticultural peat is usually taken from the oldest and deepest peat reserves, which release a huge amount of stored CO_2 into the atmosphere when dug up. There are loads of viable alternatives out there.

1. **Sandy composts** are really great for succulents and cacti as well as many bedding plants (such as pelargoniums) and Mediterranean herbs that need good drainage.
2. **Bulrush compost** is a good multipurpose product, completely renewable and (in Europe) doesn't have far to travel, making its carbon footprint relatively light.
3. **Composted sheep's wool** has a growing momentum and is highly rated as a comparable alternative to peat. It is totally renewable and requires few air miles.
4. **Coir products** are very popular. As a by-product of the coconut industry, they are fairly sustainable, but the associated deforestation of tropical rainforests in order to grow the coconuts in the first place makes this a less sustainable product.
5. **Soil-based composts** are really reliable and create strong plants that will adapt quickly once in the ground. However, they are heavy, so less eco-friendly in transit, and can be prone to waterlogging.
6. **Local authority compost** made from green waste and homemade compost are really good products – cheap or even free to make and high in nutrients – but they can contain a lot of weed seed unless sterilized, which, of course, reduces their 'green' credentials.

Homemade compost

This is a great way to reduce your impact on the environment while keeping your garden and, in particular, its soil in tip-top condition. You can put most garden waste on a compost heap. Too much grass will turn to sludge, but a little is great to increase nitrogen levels. Leaves can be included with other compost materials or added to a separate bin to make leafmould, a rich material that helps to bind the soil. Small twigs and charred wood are great for the compost heap (usually no thicker than a finger), or shred or chip woody material to get it smaller. For a healthy compost heap:

1. Start with a little soil or compost in the base, as this will contain much-needed microbes to get things started.
2. Try to avoid composting too many weed seeds and always avoid putting perennial weed roots in the compost heap. These can survive the composting process and be troublesome later on.
3. Do not put cooked food or meat in the compost, as the smell will usually attract rats.
4. The smaller the material, the quicker it will break down.
5. Make sure the heap is kept a little moist.
6. Remember that composting is carried out by living things: bacteria, fungi, wasps, flies, maggots, bugs and all kinds of creatures. Having a compost heap will give a home to all of these species, many of which will help by reducing pest numbers in your garden.
7. Turn it regularly, moving the contents of one bin into another to mix.
8. Be very careful before disturbing a compost heap, as it could harbour lovely lizards, mammals and even snakes and spiders – some of which, in certain countries, can have a nasty bite!
9. Compost generates heat as it rots – some is needed to get things moving but if it gets too hot, the rotting process can slow. This is another reason to turn the heap every few months.
10. Use your compost in the late winter or spring, or in very cold areas in the autumn, as a thick mulch on the soil. This will protect your fragile plants as well as feeding the ground without digging, ready for the year ahead.
11. Look into new and innovative composting systems like bokashi, compost tumblers and wormeries, all of which produce high-intensity feed for your plants as a by-product.
12. As well as making traditional compost, try making biochar (see page 99), which is great for slowly releasing accessible nutrients, reducing smells and helping soil structure and water retention.
13. Compost tea is a great liquid feed for plants and can be made with a range of materials such as nettles, comfrey, weeds and tithonia (in tropical regions). Simply soak the plant matter in water for a few weeks or months and dilute the liquid to feed your plants as you water (see page 101).

Watering regimes

This is an important consideration, especially in increasingly unpredictable climates. We use such a lot of water and it is a resource that is by no means infinite. Only 1 per cent of the world's water is clean and drinkable and it seems such a waste to use it on plants when rain readily falls from the sky in many areas and does the job just as well. Here are some ideas for reducing water wastage:

— Consider some of the amazing and innovative ways of harnessing water, including SUDs (sustainable urban drains), grey water recycling, reed beds, water butts and rain gardens.

— Choose perennial plants, plant them in the right place and establish them well to reduce their future watering needs.

— Water plants rarely, but water them well. This encourages them to grow strong and deep roots, making them far less likely to dry out in the increasingly hot, dry spells, as they are able to access water from deep in the ground.

— Gather and collect storm water from flooding for use later. Boreholes, wells and reservoirs can do this, but try creating channels and ditches, even using upturned umbrellas, to funnel water into tanks as an effective water-saving solution.

— In the event of excessive rainfall, trees and floodplain species can provide a great way of soaking up flood water to avoid flash floods.

Garden maintenance

To maintain a garden in an eco-friendly way requires thoughtful planning of layout and material choices (see page 32). A lumpy, bumpy lawn, for example, will probably require a mechanical cut but you might think about creating a perfectly flat lawn that could be cut with a push mower that requires no power other than your own arms. At every point of maintenance, try to cut out big, motorized machinery, reduce your chemicals and even reduce your maintenance so that areas are allowed to go a little wild, giving extra benefit to wildlife. That could mean leaving some twigs and leaves on the ground, or only mowing your lawn once a year, letting a few weeds slip through the net, or leaving a patch completely undisturbed for years at a time.

Meadow full of ox-eye daisies (*Leucanthemum vulgare*) under fruit trees

Plastics

From fake grass to plastic pots, seed trays, packaging and (heaven forbid) plastic plants, our gardens have been reliant on plastic in recent decades. The greatest offender is the plastic flower pot. However, there is some progress: the ubiquitous black plastic pot, which cannot be recycled, is slowly being replaced by a grey/taupe alternative that industrial recycling machinery can recognise and process.

There are some recycling and reuse schemes at garden centres, but some problems still need addressing. Most garden centres do not grow their own stock but buy in from wholesalers, so have very little or no use for plastic pots. Before they can be reused, pots need to go through a cleaning and sterilization process to avoid spreading pathogens, like flat worms or *Xylella fastidiosa*, around the country or the world. This sterilization incurs a cost, both environmental and financial.

Plastic pots are perfectly suited to their job: they are lightweight, provide good drainage and are cheap to manufacture if they break. Plants are generally happy in them. They are not good conductors of heat so roots don't quickly overheat or freeze, and the flexible sides make removing and repotting plants a fairly simple process. All of these issues must be addressed before alternatives can be considered – not just by the gardener, but by global and national policy and by the industry. An awareness of these issues by amateur gardeners, though, does get people thinking, and a collective consciousness and campaigning can lead to change, or pressure for change, as well as innovative solutions.

In the meantime, I try to reduce the amount of plastic pots I buy and I reuse old pots in the garden and on the allotment when I propagate. There are some alternatives that nurseries are beginning to use and I always try to buy these to show the demand is there. These alternatives include:

1. Cardboard – not very long-lasting and does involve deforestation, but a good biodegradable option.
2. Coir – coconut fibre with the same drawbacks as coconut compost (see page 20), but still biodegradable and fairly lightweight.
3. Clay or terracotta – expensive, breakable and heavy for transportation. Can come in varied shapes and sizes and can stack. They also look lovely and last for years.
4. Plant-fibre pots – usually made from grains and by-products of agriculture, these are comparable to plastic. They are lightweight, stackable, so easy to transport, totally biodegradable and fairly attractive. There are a few drawbacks, though: they are prone to waterlogging, are more expensive than plastic, and they are brittle and do not bend when plants are being removed.

Whether plastic or terracotta, re-use your pots for as long as you can. They offer great space-saving options and productivity

Choosing and raising plants

Plant provenance

Even though we consider provenance when it comes to food and clothes, I have rarely heard queries about plant provenance voiced. For me this is a really huge issue. It is not unheard of for a plant to make multiple trips across the globe before it reaches our garden centres. Supermarket fruits and vegetables carry labels stating where they were grown, so we understand their carbon footprint. That is not the case with plants. As consumers, we are not able to vote with our wallets, as we don't know what we're voting for. The horticultural industry needs to be far more transparent. We should always know where plants have come from and what journey they have taken so we can make informed choices about our purchases. This includes seeds, cut flowers, dried plant material and living plants.

Rare plants and the plant trade

This is similar to plant provenance but with the added element of risk to native flora (and, by extension, fauna) in its region of origin. Some of the world's most endangered plants are the most expensive and desirable, and often sold by illicit trading. Even when buying a relatively cheap plant from nice people, you must always make enquiries as to how this plant was obtained. Was it taken from its natural habitat in the wild and, if so, is it part of a reintroduction programme in its native habitat? Plant conservation is a huge task and large botanical institutions like the Royal Botanic Gardens in Edinburgh, where I trained, work tirelessly towards conserving and reintroducing threatened species, which may have a unique and important role in their native habitat.

Lots of plant pillaging is also carried out by the pharmaceutical and cosmetic industries, and we need a global effort to enforce tighter restrictions. But as gardeners we can do our bit. We can make sure any rare plants we buy have the relevant paperwork, proving they have been collected legally and sustainably and been grown in cultivation rather than collected from the wild. And we can avoid buying rare and endangered plants illegally. But that's obvious, right?

Propagation

By producing our own plants, we not only save money and have healthy stock that will be acclimatized to our gardens and soil, but we also stand a chance of growing plants that are as carbon neutral as possible. There is an argument for maintaining genetic variation in your stock, so buy in fresh stock every now and then or grow some plants from seed rather than by vegetative cuttings (see Propagating Plants, pages 110–123).

Veg and productive gardening

This is a crucial part of being a modern gardener, and often the most desirable part for younger people and children. We can still feel an echo of the tradition of keeping edibles separate from the social or ornamental areas of a garden, but this is an antiquated practice and one that needs a rethink. I have created gardens made entirely of edibles, and just last year grew a huge amount of edibles in a tiny space, which kept me fed much more efficiently and prolifically than my whole allotment plot and (I think) looked absolutely stunning. For me, the choice between edibles or ornamentals is a false dichotomy.

Making your own products

For a few years I have used mostly products that I've made myself – moisturizer, lip balm, massage products for aching muscles, bath bombs and so on – to reduce air miles, chemicals and packaging. And that's just cosmetics. Think of all the fun to be had by also growing plants that can be turned into dyes, pigments or even fabric. You could even grow medicinal plants with a bit of research and guidance, and as long as you never take anything without first making sure it's safe.

Preserving

Whatever we grow can be preserved in a multitude of ways. This is not only enjoyable to do, but really important for saving money, reducing food waste and generally living more sustainably. I have included some lovely preserving recipes in this book, so start saving up your jars and pots now!

Varied species – natives and non-natives

Generally, the more 'native' your plants are, the more varied uses they will offer to your local wildlife, and the more easily they will grow in your climate. They will need less watering, feeding and other interventions. However, there are some arguments for growing a wide range of plants and edibles. For example, in a temperate area, if you grow tropical edibles like turmeric, lemongrass, chillies, ginger and peppers in your greenhouse or home, then you are reducing the air miles on your food shop. So native is not always necessary. When it comes to benefiting wildlife, though, native or near-native (from countries close to yours and with similar climatic conditions) will offer the most useful food sources – leaves, pollen, nectar, fruit and seed for wildlife.

Garden Design
+ Green
Thinking

2

Incorporating plants into our lives is a kind of green thinking, but gardening isn't always as green as you might hope. Cultivating the land, turning something unused into something valued, should be a good thing and in many ways it is. But, increasingly, the trend is for design led by hard landscaping: paving, gravel, raised beds, walls, fake turf and fewer actual plants.

Hard landscaping is what creates our structure, our lines, our vistas and even how we use the space. It can be rustic and sparing or it can be brutalist and bold, but whatever its visual merits, it can always be green. Indeed, with clever design there is no need to compromise on the aesthetic value of our outdoor spaces while still adhering to our green values. If we start with the basic design and approach it from the impact it will have, where our materials have come from, what they will be and how the construction will be carried out using sustainably sourced or recycled materials, we will have already got the bare bones right and the rest will follow.

Grass meadow full of *Alopecurus*

Key components of a botanically diverse, productive, green garden

1. Strong structural features – walls, fences, pathways, sculptures and shapes – that will give form and intention, no matter what nature 'decides' to do!
2. A pond – this will bring in wildlife and offer a haven for all kinds of creatures, for drinking, bathing, spawning and feeding.
3. Trees or shrubs – the 'lungs of the planet', trees and shrubs offer nesting sites, safety and shade, reduce pollution and noise and, if we choose carefully, provide fruit or nuts.
4. Useful and direct routes through the space for usability.
5. Not too many plants to maintain – be realistic about your capabilities.
6. Tucked-away corners for wildlife to hide and nest.
7. Vegetable areas to grow your own.

The impact of climate change on design

As a gardener, I get a first-hand view of how our climate is changing. In temperate areas, weather patterns are increasingly erratic; long periods of drought followed by long periods of waterlogging and more frequent wind and storms. Each year has seen record-breaking highs in heat, rain levels and droughts, and though most winters are mild, we get unseasonable and unpredictable cold snaps. In the tropics and very dry regions, climate fluctuations manifest themselves in ever more dramatic ways. This all has relevance to garden design – how we protect our gardens from the changing climate, and also how we protect the environment around our gardens. The more hard landscaping we include in our designs, the less resistant we are to things like storm water. Rain lands on the hard surfaces and so runs off into our streets and drains, sometimes undermining subterranean structures and geology, and making

floods more likely. Permeable construction – things like gravel, dry stone walls and paving infilled with sand rather than mortar – allow water to drain away. Plants themselves offer the most protection from excess water. A mature tree with a trunk of around 12cm (5in) in diameter removes about 225 litres (50 gallons) of water per day. Add to this smaller plants that can assist with water uptake and you see that you have alleviated the worst of the problem. It may be that your garden has very little rain and unrelenting sun. In recent decades, pioneers like the late Beth Chatto developed a system of 'right plant, right place' whereby you choose species that, once established (a year or two after planting), will need little or no intervention from you. So in a damp, shady spot you plant moisture-loving ferns, ivy, mosses or bog plants; and in a bright, sunny and free-draining position you create borders of Mediterranean herbs, sun-lovers or alpines. This way you save water, save work and create a self-sustaining ecosystem in your garden. A space that experiences drought in the summer and waterlogging in the winter would be best suited to plants that evolved on flood plains, which naturally experience huge seasonal variation – things like rudbeckia, helenium, hostas, grasses and iris, to name just a few.

Left: *Geum* 'Totally Tangerine' with alliums / Right: *Wisteria* has been trained to form a rain canopy above a table

Choosing hard landscaping

Some hard landscaping features change their character in different positions. A rocky wall, for instance, looks great in a dark and damp corner of the garden, colonized by moss and ferns, providing a gorgeous structure that shows off the plants you have chosen, as well as a valuable source of food and shelter for wildlife. Put that same wall in the sun, though, and you have radically altered the feature into a monolithic, arid environment, preferred by alpines and shallow-rooting herbs as well as the insects. Rocks and stone then, offer a fairly varied range in terms of design. Wood can be a little trickier. As fencing, it is hard-wearing, attractive and versatile, but as a surface underfoot, it is prone to becoming slippery when wet. Gravel, likewise, is less attractive in a very damp spot as moss and algae forms in it, and removing fallen leaves is a real challenge. So consider gravel and decking for sunnier, open areas while in darker corners, use bark or wood chip, shade-tolerant turf or meadow-grass or a moss garden. Any of these would be free-draining, eco-friendly alternatives. Construction method is also key when trying to create something beautiful that works in harmony with the environment. Using excessive concrete, tarmac, plastic or any other material that offers little drainage will increase water run-off and be tough on wildlife. Instead, place your buildings and structures, pathways and patios on free-draining materials such as hardcore and sand. Membranes beneath structures are very useful in creating a clean, minimalist look with level surfaces and straight lines, as they stop weeds from growing up through cracks and ensure there is a solid base on which your hard landscaping can sit, but use permeable, breathable textiles, as opposed to plastic ones. Most of us have the luxury of choice here, but if you have additional needs regarding access – you or a frequent visitor is a wheelchair-user, for example – then level, wide paving is a must. I recently laid a patio of reclaimed brick on bare soil, with no foundation and no weed membrane, simply levelling compacted soil in order to create a flat surface. The effect was a rustic look, with minimal environmental impacts. Any construction book would consider this bad practice, but that is where I believe modern gardeners have a different outlook. We don't see a 'right' way and a 'wrong' way of doing things, just lots of different ways. It doesn't matter how we do something, so long as we do it well and prepare for a little extra maintenance.

Sourcing materials

Sourcing your materials locally is another very important consideration. Invariably, the cheapest materials are brought in from the furthest possible regions. India exports a huge amount of sandstone, for example, and it's usually much cheaper than locally sourced alternatives. However, a garden that uses material found in its locality is always much more visually pleasing than one in which the materials in no way reflect the surrounding area. Unity creates harmony, and reflecting your regional rock and timber can be a really simple way to make your garden look part of the natural landscape.

The other obvious benefit of sourcing locally is the reduced air and sea miles and lower carbon footprint or damage to marine life. Again, tradition often dictates sourcing new bricks, stone and timber, yet reclaiming is becoming increasingly popular. Greenhouses made from old windows, walls made from old bricks, gabions filled with old wine bottles or tiles, decking and lawn edging, and rock gardens or structures built from stones dug up from the ground can be cheap, look amazing and, being bespoke, exactly fit your needs and space.

Also consider upcycling – railway sleepers as raised beds and lawn edging, containers made of tins, boxes, cases, tanks, mugs and even furniture, walls made of old bottles, paths made of old timber or stone. By thinking carefully and cleverly about your design materials you can create something unique, with a minimal carbon footprint, making your hard landscaping modern in both senses.

Right: Ivy, ferns, mosses and lichen, growing on a wall made from local stone

Hard landscaping alternatives

There is huge scope for rethinking your hard landscaping and building features that would traditionally be 'hard' out of 'soft' materials. A hedge, for example, gives the same kind of boundary as a wall or fence, but with the ability to absorb CO_2, provide a home for creatures, create wildlife corridors and provide berries and flowers for animals and pollinators. It could even offer a useful crop — try creating a hedge out of herbs for teas, tinctures, scents, cooking, cosmetics or medicine, or make a hedge from perennial vegetables, fruit trees or shrubs, or useful climbers.

And those are just options to replace a wall. A pergola — traditionally made from wood or metal — could instead be created with the natural canopy of trees. A pathway or patio, usually built from paving slabs, sets, bricks or decking, could instead include grass, ground-cover plants or even useful plants like chamomile. These can be incredibly effective when combined with permeable hard landscaping like gravel, bricks or blocks laid on hardcore rather than concrete, and interplanted with all kinds of low-growing plants.

There is also scope to replace hard-landscaping features with materials that offer permanent structure while still providing for the ecosystem — features like dead hedges, formed of twigs and other 'dead' materials, which can provide great corridors for wildlife. All kinds of varied materials — both organic, such as pine cones and twigs, and inorganic, like brick, stones, broken pots and recycled bottles — can be piled up and used as part of the construction of walls to incorporate insect homes into the very fabric of your hard landscaping.

Plants for alternative 'walls'

1. Fruits — cherry, apple (clipped or espalier), quince, blackthorn (sloe), damson, bullace (plum)
2. Small fruits — currants, raspberry, gooseberry, jostaberry, blueberry
3. Herbs for cooking — lavender, rosemary, thyme, South African rosemary (*Eriocephalus africanus*), sage, oregano, marjoram
4. Herbs for medicine — rose, lavender, myrtle (great for hedging), aloe (in mild climates), rosemary, ginkgo, willow, echinacea (herbaceous perennial)
5. Herbs for tea — *Camellia sinensis*, lemon verbena, sage, raspberry leaf, bergamot (for more on herbs, see pages 140–165)
6. Plants for wildlife — ornamental currant (*Ribes*), hawthorn, *Pyracantha*, *Chaenomeles*, rowan (*Sorbus*), whitebeam
7. Useful climbers — grape vine, kiwi, hop, passionflower, bramble, loganberry, tayberry, *Akebia quinata*, honeyberry (*Lonicera caerulea*), Japanese wineberry

Plants for alternative 'paths' and 'patios'

- *Ajuga reptans*
- chamomile
- *Erigeron karvinskianus*
- *Pachysandra terminalis*
- sedum

- *Soleirolia soleirolii* (mind-your-own-business)
- sweet woodruff
- thyme

Below: Fleabane (*Erigeron karvinskianus*) growing through a patio

Left: A medicinal herb bed of *Echinacea*, rose and fennel has been allowed to fill with wild flowers, adding to its beauty and ease of maintenance

Designing for usability and maintenance

This is a crucial consideration when thinking about any space you interact with. How will you use it? What's its purpose and what must it provide? These are the practical parameters in which you will create your design. These considerations, as well as determining how the space will be maintained in future years, become all the more pressing as the plants take on a life of their own. Remember that things do not end when the landscapers go home. These plants will grow and change. Some may die over time, others may get much bigger than you expected. Even the most experienced gardeners make mistakes with planting, so creating and implementing a design that will be manageable is critical for its long-term success.

Both function and ease of maintenance can be tackled in the initial design stages. Let me give you an example. A veg patch at the end of the garden (as tradition dictates) is a ridiculous notion, both in terms of usability and maintenance. As anyone who has ever had an allotment will tell you, maintaining annual vegetables is no mean feat. It requires the sowing of seeds, regular watering until they germinate, pricking out, planting out, thinning, feeding once a week and watering most days through the summer. Then there's the harvest, the seed saving, the clearing and composting of the spent plant material, followed by the soil prep, sowing of green manure, mulching with manure or compost, and weeding in readiness for next year. Why, oh why, would you place this most intensive of spaces at the furthest point from your house, when you'll have to traipse up and down with the hosepipe or watering cans, wheelbarrows, buckets, tools, harvesting baskets and all other sorts of things? If you place the kitchen garden by the kitchen for ease of harvest, next to the tool shed for ease of maintenance or, crucially, near the water supply, then you have saved yourself hours of to-ing and fro-ing. A careful design also means this need not be a compromise on beauty, with herbs, crops and flowers coexisting in harmony.

Permaculture

Paths

This kind of useful and sustainable guidance for design is known as permaculture. It's a buzz word that has developed some rather restrictive connotations over the years, but in essence it is just a way of designing a garden that works with nature and works with you. The parts you'll use most are nearest the house – here the land is highly cultivated, but using low-impact methods like no-dig, and sustainable drainage and watering. As the garden spreads further from the house, it is separated into zones that become incrementally lower in impact, until you get to the furthest reaches of the land, which are essentially left to go wild. As you can probably imagine, this kind of method works best on a larger scale, but that doesn't mean we can't adopt the basic concept effectively in our small gardens. If nothing else, it will save you work and help the environment by having little or no impact on the soil, creating a balanced subterranean ecosystem.

All kinds of ideas, systems and practices are encouraged in permaculture. Most of them concentrate on circular systems where compostables and waste feed back into your garden, increasing productivity while having the lowest possible carbon footprint. Methods like grey water recycling and dead hedges have all been adopted in horticulture through permaculture, as has 'hugelkultur', where mounds are built up from a mixture of green waste, charred waste, woody material, soil and compost, to create a rich and deep well of nutritional reserves on which plants can grow, their roots stabilizing the mounds.

Permaculture is designed to be inclusive, for communities, nature and landscape, as well as productive and low impact, so don't feel intimidated by its label. It's definitely worth exploring and interpreting for your garden.

Paths that are too narrow and ground that is uneven or unstable can cause massive headaches as you move around your plot, particularly if you have any young children or issues with your sight or mobility. Similarly, routes are crucial. A path that has a soft meander is a joy. One that zigzags can be intriguing, as you can't see all the way to the end and don't know what's coming. A path that takes you on an unnecessarily convoluted route, though, is a pain. And angles and bends that are too acute will cause problems when pushing a wheelbarrow, for example. Always consider these things carefully. You want a path to feel 'designed' and surprising, but without ever compromising usability, or being impractical.

Keep it simple

Many of us, myself included, are overcome by the temptation to cram as much into a garden design as possible. Don't do it. If it looks busy on paper, then it will look busy in real life. Just because something is clean and simple doesn't mean there isn't a lot going on. Let the planting tell the story. Fill the space with curves and shapes and colours you love and give them room to breathe. The clever placing of a single feature makes a huge impact.

None of this means that a garden needs to be a clinical space full of straight lines and blank spaces. Quite the opposite. A garden is inherently a living, breathing space; the most effective designs are the ones in which the plants and hard surfaces strike the right balance. Picture a low, white wall with a gravel path alongside. The wall contains a bed filled with plants. If that wall goes crisply into the gravel floor, then that's fine. Everything is contained and neat – but maybe a tad dull. Now imagine that where that wall meets the gravel, a seed has been allowed to sprout. It could be a delicate feathered fennel, or it could be a bright *Cerinthe* or *Calendula*. Either way, it looks beautiful, naturally breaking up that space.

Finally, imagine that you have created some kind of bed between the base of the wall and the gravel. Even if is small, it will need to be surrounded by some kind of barrier to stop the gravel and soil mixing, and there would be many more plants. To me this image is too busy. We don't get to appreciate the flowers in the top bed, above the wall, because the lower ones distract the eye. We don't get to appreciate that crisp, white wall either. We don't get to see the line where that wall meets the gravel, and maintenance would be a nightmare. One or two plants enhance, a whole infrastructure detracts. That is only an example but it works across the whole design: in the placement of paths, greenhouses, patios, pergolas, lawns, sheds, cold frames, raised beds, hedges, fences, trees and other plants. So be controlled and keep the basic structure simple and considered.

Right: an upcycled, galvanized water trough, filled with the foliage of a *Galium odoratum* and *Pittosporum*

Planting schemes

Now we get on to planning your planting schemes. Start by asking these questions:

1. What do I want my garden to do?
2. What can I realistically maintain?

Get these two things right and you're on to a winner.

Broadly speaking, plants fall into the following categories and it's worth remembering this when you plan your borders. I've known people spend a small fortune on plants that turn out to be annuals, and they have to restock the whole garden the following year.

- **Annual** – a plant that will grow, flower, set seed and then die in a single year.
- **Hardy annual** – a plant that will still only flower once, but the leaves might see you through a winter.
- **Biennial** – a plant that puts on leafy growth in the first year and then flowers in the second, setting seed and then dying.
- **Monocarpic** – a plant that will only flower once, then set seed and die, but that flowering may happen after 30 years. Bamboos are in this category.
- **Non-hardy perennial** – a plant that will come back year after year but only if there is no frost.
- **Hardy herbaceous perennial** – a plant that will come back and usually flower every year. They aren't as showy as annuals but often better value for money. They have green

sappy growth right down to the ground that will die right back when dormant – usually cut this off in the early spring.
- **Woody perennial** – a shrub or sub-shrub that will grow year after year. Although they might require some pruning, they will not need to be cut right back to the ground.
- **Trees and shrubs** – large woody plants with a single stem (trees) or more than one stem (multi-stem trees or shrubs) that add impact to a garden, offering a canopy and nesting space for birds, but take up a lot of groundwater.

As well as these botanical categories, it is also worth noting whether something is evergreen (retains its foliage) or deciduous (loses its leaves in winter). Usually the aim is to have one-third of a border filled with evergreen structure. Scent will also elevate a garden and turn it from a visual experience into a visceral one. Other things to consider are:

- **Productivity and use** – is the plant edible, medicinal, used as a dye plant or a cut flower?
- **Toxicity** – it's always worth noting if something is poisonous. A lot of plants that we are very familiar with as ornamentals are highly toxic if ingested, or are an irritant to the skin. Some medicinal herbs can be too if taken without knowing the exact dose or method of preparation. Always proceed with caution when eating plants and avoid plants with toxicity if you have young children, pets or livestock.

- **Use to the local wildlife** – I always try to include plants that produce fruit, flowers, seeds and material for nesting, or that can be useful for insects, pollinators, small mammals and birds in other ways. If something has a double flower rather than a single, for example, it is useless to pollinators and I tend not to buy it.

Once you have worked out what your plants' role will be in general and which ones you want to include in particular, it only remains to work out whether you will be able to maintain them. It's fairly pointless to plant up a garden you will not have time to keep on top of. In fact, you run the risk of turning something that should be a joy into a source of stress rather than relaxation. So be realistic when you are at the planning stage. What does your skill set allow – bear in mind that you will learn quickly and get better, at which point you can expand – and what does your budget and free time allow?

Right: A mixed bed of edibles, flowers, wildflowers and herbs, with a backdrop of architectural and delicious rhubarb

Community gardening

Many of us today do not have a garden. We often live with our parents for longer, or we live in small flats or shared houses with small or non-existent gardens. But we can turn to public and shared outdoor spaces for our gardening needs. I myself have an allotment, which is a lifeline and allows me to harvest my own vegetables for a lot of the year. Land sovereignty is increasingly political, but in different countries around the world, there are some really interesting and innovative ideas to enable people to access land. In areas of Northern Europe and Scandinavia, where most people live in apartments, cities provide green spaces where people can either buy or use little patches of land. The Swedish system, for example, was set up in the 1890s based on a Danish system first conceptualized a hundred years earlier. Allotment gardens are designated spaces either within or just outside towns and cites, where people can have spaces to grow whatever they like – ornamentals or crops – and erect log cabin-style homes with water and electricity, which offer an escape within the city. These kinds of communal spaces have been emulated the world over, with a similar scheme being set up in the Philippines in 2003. Community gardens, on the other hand, offer a slightly different service. Not just a place for individuals to grow on their own little plot, but a place where all kinds of people can come together to grow, eat, learn and chat. These are inherently diverse and inclusive spaces. Some of these growing initiatives are quietly welcoming while others are more active and radical. By and large, these kinds of spaces seem to grow with a 'modern' ethos of minimal impact and maximum yield. Some gardens are set up to offer respite; for those suffering with their mental or physical health, homeless people, or those struggling with addiction, for example. Many places like this also just offer a safe and respectful place for families and neighbourhoods, a place where they can meet people and learn new skills.

Guerilla gardening

Guerilla gardening, rather than working in a designated place, aims to take over unused spaces and convert them into species-rich and productive spaces that are accessible to all as they are on public land. These movements tend to be very low impact, and are usually created on shoestring budgets as there is often the risk of vandalism, or being turfed off the property. This is the movement converting existing green spaces and overlooked, public spaces into places that actively serve their communities without destroying unspoilt habitats, which the creation of public amenity spaces outside the city habitually does. The challenge is in getting people involved with growing in their community, and claiming territory by stealth, until their right to the land use is accepted by local authorities. There are, of course, public green spaces that are already in existence. Often found in large urban areas where outside space is limited, parks and nature reserves can offer a vital escape from the metropolis. Although they are beautiful and hugely beneficial to the wellbeing of the people who use them, I would argue these spaces could also benefit from a dose of 'modern gardening'. If they went a step further in benefitting local communities and wildlife, by allowing people to grow their own plants in designated areas and by adopting an environmentally sensitive maintenance regime, they could really provide a lifeline for us and other species. Budgets have a huge impact on the management of public spaces, as is always the case, but rethinking the allocation of a budget could have a far-reaching impact, especially if those in charge engage the community about what they want from their spaces: spend less on chemicals and mowers and more on gardeners who can take the time to maintain the space sympathetically. The modern garden, like the modern world, is not homogenous. It adapts according to political and environmental challenges and is accessible to all, because we realize more and more that the financial, climatic and political challenges we face have the power to unify or divide us. Outdoor spaces, especially those driven by the community, can play an enormous role in bringing us all together. Gardens and land management can improve insect and animal biodiversity and offer spaces for us to grow our own healthy food, learn about nature, boost our confidence and build on our strengths as a species. Community, cooperation, discussion, communication, empathy and sympathy together create the very essence of humanity and can be seen at their best in these wonderful shared spaces. Parks, if reorganized, can also offer a very real solution to food shortages and take some of the strain off intensive farming and

trading. An inclusive garden, whether on our windowsill, outside our back door or down the road from us, can be all of our responsibility. If we modernize our thoughts about a garden – what it is, what it does, who it benefits and how, with clever design and conservation – and an understanding of the role we play as gardeners and as human beings – we will have improved our gardens (in terms of both visual impact and productivity), and in the process we will have improved our planet's health, our community and in turn our own lives.

Houseplants

Houseplants are often described as a 'trend', but, in my opinion, they not only live in the home, they make a home. When I was a student, I had a single peace lily (*Spathiphyllum wallisii*) – it was all I could afford. I used to carry this plant with me from room to room in my dingy, shared flat in Edinburgh. Although I liked to think of myself as Léon, The Professional, the truth is I was less cool and less murderous. The room just felt ... well, nicer with the plant for company. Luckily for me, this is one of the more robust houseplants and it could cope with the heat in the kitchen, the draught in the bedroom and probably thanked me for the damp when it came into the bathroom.

This magical greening effect in the home has led to the somewhat dismissive idea that houseplants are a great home accessory. Of course they can be, but they are also living, complex organisms, fascinating life forces, air purifiers, sources of potential food, amazing air fresheners and friends. Remember, though, most houseplants are tropical and from far-flung places, so you need to consider things like air miles, sustainable harvesting, in-situ global conservation and illegal trade, opting for locally propagated stock if possible.

Previous page: *Monstera adansonii*

Right: Shade-loving maidenhair fern (*Adiantum raddianum*), edible taro (*Colocasia esculenta*) and *Monstera adansonii*

If I'm being honest...

Growing houseplants can be quite advanced horticulture. More than anything else (except how to get rid of slugs and snails), people ask me why they always kill their houseplants. It's a common problem, and it took me many years of practice and failures (otherwise called learning experiences) to get the hang of houseplants.

Common houseplant blunders

1. Buying bad plants

Supermarkets, homeware stores and department stores often have a section for houseplants. They're cheap, they're tempting, they have come from who-knows-where and they're often doomed. Very few plants I have purchased from these shops have ever done well; even the succulents, which by rights require little to no care. They've often had a long journey through different temperatures, varying light levels, irregular care and a healthy dose of foliar feed to keep them looking good in the short term. They may have hardly even had time to root and, most worryingly, we may not even know what they are. So often I see plants labelled as 'foliage', which of course covers roughly 100% of the plants in the world, so you end up with no idea what the aftercare should be. Buy from specialist nurseries, ask about the care of the plant, where it's come from, how it's been grown and how it should be treated from here on.

2. Not knowing what you have

Caring for any plant you don't know is really hard. You should know exactly what you're buying, both inside and outside your home. The genus (that's the first bit of the botanical name, like *Spathiphyllum*) tells you a lot about what the plant is and, very roughly, what kind of conditions it needs. However, some genera are very widespread and contain numerous plants requiring very different conditions, so it's really helpful to know the species name too. For example, it's *wallisii*. The 'ii' just means 'named after Mr (it's usually a Mr) Wallis'. Often, though, the species name will give you some horticultural information – for example, *japonica* means 'comes from Japan', *sylvestris* means 'from woodland' and *multiflora* means 'lots of flowers'.

These botanical names also save confusion, as common names vary from region to region. Everyone in the world uses the same botanical name, and as many houseplants come from exotic climes, it guarantees you're getting the right thing and makes researching their preferred conditions much easier.

3. Thinking it's one-size-fits-all

It isn't. A house plant is simply a plant that will be happy in your home. It may love to be kept really dry and warm like a cactus, it may like bright conditions like most succulents, it may like shady, cooler conditions like a lot of tropical ferns and forest flora (usually with large leaves), it may like to be kept in a very moist atmosphere like lots of orchids and air plants. It may prefer to be outside in the summer, like gingers, or need extra protection from pests, like chillies. Always choose an appropriate spot.

4. Bringing outdoor plants indoors

This really is a big no no. Plants that often suffer from this kind of treatment are things like Bonsai (or Penjing in China), which are notoriously challenging to grow. If an outdoor plant gets put indoors it simply will not survive. So if a plant is happy in your garden, don't bring it inside.

5. Choosing the wrong indoor climate

Light, heat, moisture, ventilation. Within our homes the conditions vary hugely; the darkest place is probably right under the window, where the sun's rays never reach and any fruiting plant like a chilli will not have the light levels to ripen fruits. Ironically, on the nearby windowsill there may be near-constant, scorching light that few plants like cacti, succulents and Pelargoniums can tolerate, especially when combined with the cold glass of the window at night. Above a radiator it will be very hot and very dry but also very variable when the heating is switching on and off throughout the day. The bathroom is invariably the moistest atmosphere; the bedroom is the best place for succulents and cacti that open their pores and cleanse the atmosphere at night rather than during the day; and the best place for the vast majority of house plants is somewhere cool and constant. Even tropical plants will find this easier to adapt to than constantly changing conditions. Think about your home's individual rooms and apply the 'right plant right place' methodology.

6. Pathogens and pests

In warm homes pathogens are more likely, and also much more of a nuisance to the human inhabitants, too! The spores of mildew and the pesky presence of flies and mites can even be a source of ill health. Once a pest or pathogen gets in (often brought in on new houseplants so always give new additions a thorough health check) they can move around quickly and spread to previously unaffected plants. A house has a warm and still atmosphere that allows nasties to spread quickly, exacerbated by the lack of natural predators to keep numbers under control as they would in the garden. The solution is diligence and a little fresh air. The last thing you want to do is fill your home with chemicals, so regularly check plant-health, remove any pests, diseased leaves or even whole plants that have been infested as soon as you find them. Take them outside, wash them thoroughly with warm, soapy water, sometimes even washing off all the compost and cleaning the roots before repotting and bringing them back in. Taking plants outside for the warmest months of the year can also be really helpful in giving them a dose of fresh air; as necessary for plants as it is for us!

7. The wrong care regime

Although we tend to blame ourselves for 'things that go wrong', mostly we look after our plants as well as we can, but the above problems make our lives difficult. With good plants, that we can correctly identify, give the right conditions and regularly check for pests and diseases, the only things left for us to do is water, prune, occasionally feed and repot them as required. Just be careful not to over water, as this is one of the biggest killers of houseplants.

For shade

Shade-loving houseplants are usually tropical plants. They have generally evolved on the forest floor in warm regions of the world and include all sorts, from ferns to flowering plants. Usually, the defining feature of a shade-loving plant (both in and outdoors) is its large leaves. In the wild, in shadier habitats a larger leaf will evolve, increasing the surface area in order to capture what little light is available. You will also find that a lot of shade-loving plants are climbers. This is another adaptation, which enables them to get to the light at the top of the canopy.

Most (though not all) shade-lovers like moisture. A large leaf means lots of water is lost through transpiration, so choose a moisture-retentive growing medium that is rich in nutrients. The best options are coir, bulrush, composted sheep's wool and sustainably sourced moss. And if you're making your own compost, use plenty of leafmould to mimic the leaf litter that surrounds these plants in their natural habitat. Remember that in the tropics there are no seasons, so it will pay dividends to maintain a temperature that's as near to constant as you can.

SHADE-LOVING PLANTS

— *Alocasia*
— *Asparagus setaceus* (asparagus fern
    – not a true fern)
— *Aspidistra* (cast-iron plant)
— *Calathea*
— *Chlorophytum* (spider plant)
— *Cissus* (grape ivy)
— *Ctenanthe*
— *Dracaena*
— *Epipremnum* (devil's ivy)
— *Ficus* (various figs)
— *Monstera* (Swiss cheese plant)
— *Peperomia*
— *Philodendron*
— *Polyscias* 'Fabian'
— *Rhapis excelsa* (lady palm)
— *Sansevieria* (mother-in-laws' tongue)
— *Zamioculcas* (ZZ plant)

SHADE-LOVING FERNS

— *Adiantum* (maidenhair fern)
— *Asplenium* 'Crissie' (bird's nest fern)
— *Asplenium nidus* 'Campio'
— *Asplenium nidus* 'Crispy Wave' (pleated
    bird's nest)
— *Asplenium* 'Osaka'
— *Asplenium* 'Parvati' (mother fern)
— *Nephrolepis* (Boston fern)
— *Phlebodium aureum* 'Blue Star' (blue star fern)
— *Platycerium bifurcatum* (staghorn fern)

Right: *Hoya carnosa* and *Asplenium* 'Parvati' / Left: *Phlebodium aureum* 'Blue Star'

For sun

Although many houseplants can cope with sunny conditions and have adapted to them in their own native environments, remember that the conditions in our homes can be variable and extreme. Few houseplants will thank you for a sunny windowsill, really hot by day and chilly by night, and most are much happier on a bright table away from magnified sunlight through glass. Plants like to take everything slowly, and the conditions in our houses can change very quickly. Minimizing temperature shock will allow your houseplants to cope in the unnatural conditions of the great indoors! Also, remember that cacti and succulents are two different things. Succulents need a surprising amount of water in the summer and very little in the winter, and most like high light levels. Cacti need hardly any water at all. Overwatering either of these, will result in damp conditions that are perfect for common pests like sciarid flies. Be on the lookout for aphids like mealy bugs, and deal with them straight away to avoid devastation.

SUN-LOVING PLANTS

— *Aeonium arboreum*
— *Agave*
— *Aloe*
— *Argyroderma testiculare* (living stones)
— *Beaucarnea* (pony tail palm)
— *Cereus forbesii*
— *Ceropegia*
— *Crassula ovata* (jade or money plant)
— *Crassula x rupestris f. marnieriana* 'Hottentot'
— *Echeveria elegans*
— *Echinocactus grusonii* (golden barrel cactus)
— *Epiphyllum anguliger* (fishbone cactus)
— *Euphorbia lactea* (coral cactus)
— *Euphorbia trigona* (African milk tree)
— *Faucaria tigrina* (tiger jaws)
— *Haworthia*
— *Humata tyermannii* (white rabbit foot fern)
— *Kalanchoe tomentosa* (panda plant)
— *Lithops pseudotruncatella* (living stones)
— *Opuntia* (prickly pear)
— *Pachyphytum bracteosum*
— *Pilosocereus gounellei*
— *Rhipsalis heteroclada* (mistletoe cactus)
— *Sedum burrito*
— *Sedum morganianum*
— *Senecio*

Left: Asparagus fern (*Asparagus setaceus*), not truly a fern at all / Right: Spannish Moss (*Tillandsia usneoides*)

For moisture-rich atmospheres

The bathroom or wet room, where light levels are low but moisture levels very high, is a great place for some houseplants. There are a few plants perfectly adapted to such a spot and some will even appreciate joining you in the shower! Many of these plants will have aerial roots evolved for obtaining moisture and nutrients, while others, including air plants, obtain their moisture and nutrients from the atmosphere through their leaves and stems. All these plants make a great addition to the bathroom and can be hung on the shower door, shower curtain pole or hooks in the walls, turning your bathroom into a veritable jungle.

Moisture-loving orchids

Orchids are perhaps the most efflorescent plants that enjoy a humid spot, but many orchids are extremely rare so care needs to be taken when buying them to ensure they have been responsibly sourced. Moth orchids (*Phalaenopsis*) are the most common orchids sold as houseplants and probably the easiest to care for; slipper orchids (*Paphiopedilum*) and pansy orchids (*Miltoniopsis*) require really humid conditions to thrive. *Oncidium* produces lots of flowers when it's happy but needs cool nights to do really well. *Zygopetalum* is truly epiphytic and doesn't require compost to grow, taking all its moisture from the air.

MOISTURE-LOVING PLANTS

— *Adiantum* (maidenhair fern)
— *Alocasia* – drier soil but moist atmosphere
— *Asparagus setaceus* (asparagus fern)
— bamboo
— bromeliads – water into the rosette
— *Chlorophytum* (spider plant) – moist soil
— *Colocasia* (taro) – moist soil
— *Cymbopogon citratus* (lemongrass)
— ferns
— *Monstera* (Swiss cheese plant) – moist soil
— *Philodendron* – moist soil
— *Tillandsia* (air plants)
— *Tillandsia usneoides* (Spanish moss)

MOISTURE-LOVING ORCHIDS

— *Miltoniopsis* (pansy orchid)
— *Oncidium*
— *Paphiopedilum* (slipper orchid)
— *Phalaenopsis* (moth orchid)
— *Zygopetalum*

Edible houseplants

Edibles are often relegated to the 'working' part of the garden, but they can bring beauty and practical value when grown indoors. The options are numerous; perfect if you enjoy cooking with new and interesting flavours. Be aware of the natural habitats of your edible houseplants, as this will, of course, determine their preferred growing conditions within the home. If a plant is tropical, give it shade and moisture; if it comes from an arid region, give it sun and don't overwater it. Many edible houseplants will crop and fruit and therefore require some feeding. This will usually be a liquid feed in the home. The edibles chapter has in-depth advice (see pages 62–109).

Some edible plants can be propagated at home. Turmeric and ginger, for example, can be grown from shop-bought rhizomes, and plants can be raised from the top of a pineapple. Sugar canes must be raised each year from cuttings, as they won't survive the winter, even indoors. Lemongrass from the supermarket will sprout roots in water.

Edible houseplants

— Aubergine
— Avocado
— Black pepper
— Cassava
— Chillies
— Cucamelon
— Ginger
— Lemongrass
— Malabar spinach
— Melon
— Okra
— Pineapple
— Rice
— Sorghum
— Squash and luffa
— Sugar cane
— Taro
— Tomato
— Turmeric
— Vietnamese coriander
— Wasabi
— Water chestnut
— Yam

Herbs

Most herbs, with the exception of basil perhaps, will be much happier outside, but if you have a windowsill by an open window, they can live happily indoors for a while. For an in-depth look at herbs, see chapter 7.

INDOOR HERBS

— Basil
— Coriander (leaves and seeds)
— Mint
— Oregano
— Parsley
— Rosemary
— Thyme

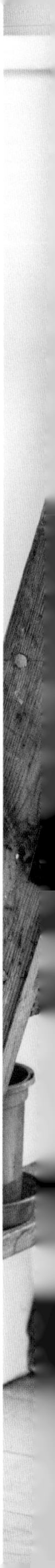

Aubergine, malabar spinach and tomatoes growing from seed

Bonsai

These plants are for the truly brave and advanced grower. Even I struggle with bonsai, simply because trees generally do not like being indoors. It's always a good idea to give your bonsai a dose of fresh air on warm summer days. And remember to buy bonsai from really expert growers who can advise you about their treatment and ensure success, as they can be a big investment and it is heartbreaking when they fail. Some bonsai will want to live outside all the time, so do bear that in mind when you're choosing your species. Prune mainly at the roots, and water by soaking the rootball regularly so that the whole base is submerged.

Houseplants and sustainability

Once you've got through the minefield of buying your plants, taking plant health and the global plant trade into consideration, you're pretty much there in terms of sustainability. The main thing to consider is that in the vast majority of cases, houseplants are grown in pots, so choose a good, peat-free compost when repotting them. The other thing to remember is that houseplants need feeding, as do any plants that live in pots. Making your own compost tea out of comfrey or nettles is a really great way of providing a low-impact plant food (see page 101). Alternatively, go for organic options like seaweed feed or bonemeal (which is animal-based, so vegans will need to look at alternatives).

A Space to Grow, Eat + Preserve

I love the idea that we can be self-sufficient in veg from a relatively small space: that something I grow can feed myself, my family, friends and the community. There is something profoundly gratifying about producing something of tangible value. Not just the personal kind of value that can be attributed to anything we have grown and nurtured, but a real, economic value. The rewards of growing plants that feed the soul and nourish the body are vast. This, I believe, is primal, and why there are so many of us; both the allotment stalwarts and the new generation.

Good food has become more a part of our everyday culture. We readily embrace cuisine from all over the world. We value food for its flavour, its nutritional value and its diversity. Modern gardeners want to replicate this in our kitchen gardens. We also want to save ourselves money and reduce our waste by ensuring we have vegetables and fruit we've grown for as much of the year as possible. This is why preserving of all kinds, from pickling to fermenting, has resurfaced.

Too many environmental battles to fight can seem overwhelming. Living a balanced life that creates minimal negative impacts on the world around us is the dream, of course, but we need not spend our time consumed by guilt for what we can't control. Just growing a little of our diet ourselves, eating seasonally and with full knowledge of where and how our food was grown seems a good place to start.

Maximizing production and minimizing impact

The traditional vegetable garden is an intensive beast; the ground is worked and reworked every year. We now understand the balance of the ecosystem and how heavy interventions in the soil can hugely disrupt the natural processes of the subterranean layer, making survival for plants, fungi and animals more challenging. That makes digging the soil and working it to the extent we have been taught to do less and less appealing, and many people are turning to no-dig methods (see page 105).

On a similar note, we also understand now that introducing chemicals, both in pest control and fertilizer, may have short-term benefits for our produce, but the long-term impact is detrimental, not only to our kitchen gardens, but to the wider ecosystem, locally and globally. We all recognize that without insects, many of our crops would go unpollinated and we would go hungry. Therefore, conserving them is an imperative and chemical pesticides are quite literally overkill.

Improving our soils while retaining moisture and nutrients can be achieved by top dressing with a mulch of compost, rotted manure or evergreen material like hay, dried weeds or nitrogen-rich leaves. This breaks down and is naturally incorporated into the soil by soil organisms to improve the structure and nutrient content.

Japanese wineberry (*Rubus phoenicolasius*)

Companion planting

In the kitchen garden, companion planting is an invaluable resource. In its simplest form (companion planting can get very complicated), it involves planting flowers alongside our vegetables and fruits to attract pollinating insects, shield plants from hungry birds, rabbits and invertebrates, and provide homes for ground beetles, ladybirds, parasitoid wasps and other predatory insects. The more varied companion plants you have, the more insects you can provide for — think nesting and basking sites for butterflies and moths, and nectar-rich plants for bees and flies.

Non-edible companion plants to attract insects

— *Artemisia* (wormwood)
— *Centaurea cyanus* (cornflower)
— *Lamium* (deadnettle)
— *Limnanthes douglasii* (poached egg plant)
— *Papaver* (poppy)
— *Phacelia*
— *Vicia* (vetch)

Edible companion plants to attract insects

— borage
— *Calendula* (pot marigold)
— chives
— fennel
— hyssop
— lavender
— linseed
— nasturtium
— parsley
— *Stellaria media* (chickweed)
— sunflower
— thyme

Left: Pot marigold (*Calendula officinalis*) / Right: Borage (*Borago officinalis*)

The other aspect to companion planting is making sure you grow beneficial crops alongside each other that take different nutrients from the soil, so you don't end up with any one nutrient being depleted. Here are a few key tips to help you get your head around the myriad combinations you can grow together:

1. Root crops (carrots, parsnips, turnips, beetroot, swede, celeriac, cassava and radish) use up phosphates in the soil. So avoid growing lots of root crops together, as it can cause a depletion of natural phosphates.

2. Anything in the bean or pea family (peas, beans, broad beans, soya beans, butter beans, wild peas, gorse, broom, clover, birds' foot trefoil) fix nitrogen in the soil with little nodules on their roots. Therefore, planting any nitrogen-hungry crop (such as brassicas and leafy veg like chard and sweetcorn) immediately after or alongside peas or beans will be beneficial to the nitrogen-hungry crop.

3. Plants grown for their fruits or seeds (currants and berries, cucumbers, tomatoes, chillies, aubergines and squashes) require more potash than other plants, so should be grown with nitrogen-hungry leafy vegetables or phosphate-hungry roots for best effect. All of this goes alongside appropriate feeds and, of course, as many insect-attracting flowers as you can fit in.

4. Consider forest gardening (see page 105) and using vertical as well as horizontal spaces. This is not companion planting in the traditional sense, but involves combining plants to provide natural supports for those with different growth habits.

5. Some planting combinations will protect certain crops from pests. A classic example is growing members of the garlic family alongside your carrots, as the strong smell of the garlic will stop carrot root fly from smelling the carrots.

Perennial crops

Many perennial crops like rhubarb, asparagus, artichokes, all kinds of berries and currants, Welsh onions and herbs are old familiars. Or well-known tropical perennials like ginger, turmeric and citrus fruits, which all need winter protection. Growing less common, though often very ancient, perennial veg could hold the key to sustainable food production on a wider scale. Agronomists are looking at how perennial crops could save water and fertilizer, preserve the soil microbiome and allow for year-round harvesting. The extensive range of available plants includes leafy substitutions for spinach or kale, onion alternatives and plants with edible roots and rhizomes.

Perennial roots

Oca (*Oxalis tuberosa*) – a member of the clover group, this plant has tangy, sour leaves for salad, and edible tubers that can replace potatoes. It originates in South America. This particular plant is from the Andes, and its montane evolution has given it a toughness that sees it through a temperate winter.

American groundnut (*Apios americana*) – with a natural range from Canada to Florida, this plant was used as a staple crop by the indigenous peoples of North America. It is now farmed commercially in Japan. It is a beautiful tender climber, with delicious, nutty tubers.

Cassava (*Manihot esculenta*) – native to South America, this shrub produces long, strong, edible (and tasty) roots. This is a tropical plant so will need to be grown in a greenhouse in temperate climates. Nigeria is at present the world's largest producer. This must be soaked and cooked before eating.

Skirret (*Sium sisarum*) – a member of the carrot family, skirret is best thought of as a perennial parsnip. It's fully hardy and will get bigger each year. This has been a popular vegetable throughout history, documented since medieval times and especially trendy during the Tudor period. A few hundred years and relative obscurity hasn't stood in the way of its endurance and now it's gaining in popularity.

Mashua (*Tropaeolum tuberosum*) a stunning South American root vegetable with edible leaves

Sweet potato (*Ipomoea batatas*) – a really common vegetable to buy but not often considered for growing. It is not hardy and so needs to be overwintered indoors, or grown in frost-free regions, but for those who have the right place for it, sweet potato is a very nutritious, lush and beautiful choice.

Jerusalem artichoke (*Helianthus tuberosus*) – this has a questionable reputation, mainly due to its high levels of inulin (associated with flatulence) and a flavour that divides opinion. Yet these plants are very prolific, ridiculously easy to grow, and delicious. Aficionados of botanical Latin will recognize that the generic name is the same as that of sunflowers, which they resemble, making them edible, beautiful and simultaneously beneficial to pollinators.

Chinese artichoke (*Stachys affinis*) – is not related to the Jerusalem artichoke, yet is similar in appearance and function. It has tall stems with purple flowers and lovely tubers that should be harvested in the autumn and eaten fresh as they do not store well. In Chinese medicine, they are used to cure colds and chest infections.

Earthnut pea (*Lathyrus tuberosus*) – the Fabaceae family contains some of the world's most commonly grown commercial crops, including soya beans, fava beans, peas, chickpeas and many more. Not many are perennial, but this one is. This groundnut-producing plant is a close relative of vetch, so, in temperate climates, it serves a really important function for pollinating insects – specifically bees.

Horseradish (*Armoracia rusticana*) – this is a great root for those with a penchant for fiery food. If it likes your soil, it will grow well – to the point where it can become a thug. I have found

it struggles with drought and full sun, though, so can be a little fussy. To keep it under control you'll be harvesting more than you can eat.

Yakon (*Smallanthus sonchifolius*) – a statuesque and dramatic plant, which is popular in Asia and Australasia, yakon comes in a range of different cultivars, but each produces large tubers. A versatile food source, it can be eaten raw or cooked, and can be turned into syrup and stored for a long time. It can cope with a gentle frost, which is thought to improve the flavour, but will not cope with extreme cold. Digging them up to harvest in the autumn allows you to store them in a frost-free spot over winter.

Mashua (*Tropaeolum tuberosum*) – this is one of my favourite plants in terms of its appearance. I love nasturtiums anyway (which are in the same genus) but to find a perennial relation, more striking and equally edible, was a revelation. They aren't easy to get hold of. Store them in a frost-free spot over winter. I tend to grow them in a large pot for ease of moving them around. Plant them deep for extra tubers.

Perennial greens

Sea beet (*Beta vulgaris maritima*) – although related to beetroot, this plant is cropped for its foliage, which tastes like spinach or chard. It grows wild, so canny coastal foragers can save themselves the growing space.

Malabar spinach (*Basella alba*) – very useful for saving space, this climbing perennial is tender, so needs winter protection. But it is lush, tasty and resplendent, making it a highly sought-after crop.

Good King Henry (*Chenopodium bonus-henricus*) – another spinach substitute, but this one is far more traditional. Like skirret, good King Henry had its heyday centuries ago, but is now regaining its former popularity. It's a relative of the Caribbean crop callaloo, though this is perennial. It does not like to be transplanted, so pick a sunny spot for it and leave it be.

Causcasian spinach (*Hablitzia tamnoides*) – this plant has gained huge popularity. It's hardy, it's beautiful and it climbs, so it's easy to care for and takes up very little space. In addition to this, *Hablitzia* can cope with some shade. It is the perfect plant to use in a forest gardening scheme to maximize productive space.

Perennial kales – there are loads of cultivars to choose from. These plants are resilient, prolific and provide nearly year-round harvesting potential. Both kale and tree collards take incredibly well from cuttings, meaning once you have one, you can easily propagate more and share them with your friends.

Tree collards – similar to kale, but on a larger scale and really, really useful as a form of edible hedging or an edible shrub, for those who want to make every space usable or subscribe to forest-gardening methods.

Hops (*Humulus lupulus*) – better known for their use in brewing, hops can also be enjoyed as an alternative to asparagus. In hop production, only three of the new bines (individual growing stems) are trained in each year to produce flowers. The rest of the emerging shoots are cut off at the base in the spring. These shoots are edible when young and tender. Don't throw them away!

Sea kale (*Crambe maritima*) – this plant has lovely leaves that can be cooked with butter, and a mass of flowers that turn to pea-like seeds. Sea kale is a really useful plant to grow. It has strong, fleshy and very deep roots developed to cling on, even in the shifting sands and shingle of the beaches where it evolved. It is also highly ornamental.

Sea kale (*Crambe maritima*) with delicious, succulent leaves and flowers that turn to pea-like, salty fruits

The onion family

Welsh onion (*Allium fistulosum*) – a thick-stemmed perennial spring onion with pretty flowers, which remains green virtually all year round. It has a mild, chive-like flavour and can be used in salads and stir-fries. Sow from seed or buy a pot and leave to form a lovely clump.

Scallion (*Allium cepa* 'Perutile') – traditional in Ireland and the Caribbean (as a key ingredient for jerk), scallion is a powerfully oniony plant which resembles a robust chive. A friend broke off four little pieces for me a few years ago and I now have more scallions than I know what to do with – and so does everyone I know. They form a thick clump quickly and can be divided really simply and reliably.

Walking onion (*Allium cepa* Proliferum Group) – a leek that flowers, flops and then regrows from wherever the flowers hit the ground. You'll need a lot of space but, for novelty value alone, these are a must-have. Wasps are also very partial to a leek flower, and although this may not sound like something to encourage, wasps have a really important function in the food chain, as decomposers and predators for pests.

Siberian chive (*Allium nutans*) – the onion family (Alliaceae) is arguably one of the most handsome, and I would personally argue that Siberian chives are the most attractive of the bunch. They are delicate, fairly low growing, but with fine, strappy leaves and an absolutely beautiful flower, beloved by bees.

Wild garlic (*Allium ursinum*) – a bit of a thug, it has to be said, but I will include this just in case anybody is struggling with a shady spot. There aren't many foods that will grow in the deepest shade, but wild garlic will. Its white flowers will add a beautiful cheer. Best harvested before it has flowered, wild garlic is a versatile plant with a strong and distinct flavour.

Chives (*Allium schoenoprasum*) – a classic choice for a herb garden, common chives are lovely. Their purple flower heads, like little lollipops, give a cottage-garden appearance, while providing food and pollen aplenty for the bees.

Society garlic (*Tulbaghia violacea*) – the word that best sums up this plant is exquisite. Originating in South Africa, where it's more often used as a snake deterrent than a food source, due to its pungent aroma, it has gained popularity the world over, and can now be found in the most upmarket restaurants as a garnish that certainly packs a punch. A little frost tender, protect this in the winter months and eat with caution – it's powerful stuff that you'll taste on your breath for hours.

Other perennial crops

Globe artichoke (*Cynara cardunculus*) – like most thistles, this is a member of the daisy family (Asteraceae). It produces large, silver, spiky leaves and grows over 1m (3ft) in a single season. The large, fleshy globes of flowers, which are its namesake, are used in traditional Mediterranean cuisine. Either harvest and eat the flowers before they fully open, or let them open and leave them for pollinators, who absolutely love them.

Asparagus (*Asparagus officinalis*) – it takes a little investment, both in money and in time, to get a good crop of asparagus. Buy crowns from a reputable nursery and plant in rich soil (though in the wild they will happily grow at the base of trees so can cope with a little competition). Do not start harvesting them until their third year of growth, and give them a mulch each winter to keep weeds down and provide nutrition. Some people prefer the thicker male plants and others prefer the seed-producing females, so if you have a preference, decide before you buy. Harvest through the spring and then let the plants grow for the rest of the year and build up strength. The spears will grow into gorgeous, delicate plants, about 1m (3ft) in height.

Rhubarb (*Rheum* x *hybridum*) – grand, statuesque and versatile, rhubarb has been a staple of the garden and allotment for many a year. Like asparagus, do not over-harvest it, but leave some stems to grow through the summer and build strength. The stems have a tart quality that can be used in savoury or sweet dishes, but the leaves are poisonous so don't eat those.

Left: Asparagus hedge / Right: Rhubarb harvest

Mandy Barber owns and manages a project in Devon, UK, called Incredible Vegetables. She is a researcher of perennial edible plants, a budding plant breeder and seed saver, and runs a small permaculture plant nursery. She is passionate about researching sustainable food crops that have built-in resilience, and wild edibles that have the potential to become future staple foods. Incredible Vegetables aims to create a diverse botanical reserve of useful edible plants, and Mandy has an ever-increasing list, including all kinds of perennial edible roots, shoots, tubers and rhizomes, leafy greens and alliums. Her growing space is a diverse polyculture of perennials, annuals, self-sowing edibles and plants for pollinators. Wildflowers work alongside an abundance of 'edimentals' and perennial vegetables in a beautiful 'food glade', a haven for all kinds of life. I have taken a lot of inspiration and learnt a lot about perennial vegetables from Mandy.

Basic jam recipe

Jam is a classic way of preserving fruit and tastes delicious in desserts, on toast or pastries or even spooned over breakfast cereal. Jam-making is quite an art form and takes a little perfecting and a few specialist tools – like a big jam pan – but it's worth a try. Jam can be made using any fruit, from plums to berries, citrus fruits and even bananas (I once had this in Cape Verde when visiting my sister, who lived there, and it is absolutely delicious). I learned jam-making from my dad, who is really keen on it and loves making quince jelly (though it's not my favourite, I have to say!). This recipe can be used for any summer berries.

Makes 3 x 450g (1lb) jars

1kg (2lb 4oz)
    summer berries

1kg (2lb 4oz) jam sugar,
    or just a little less

a squeeze of lemon juice

1. Rinse the fruits, halving any large ones. Place in a large bowl with the sugar, stir well and leave overnight to allow the sugar to start dissolving.
2. The next day, place a plate or dish in the freezer.
3. Place the fruit, sugar and lemon juice into a large pan and slowly bring it to the boil. This usually takes about 20 minutes.
4. Once it's boiling, start to test the jam by spooning a little drizzle onto the chilled plate. If the surface wrinkles when gently pushed, then it's ready. If not, boil for a little longer and test again.
5. Pour the jam into sterilized jars, cover with circles of waxed paper to keep the air out and close the lids while the jam is still hot. It should keep for years.

Perennial fruit

Pears (*Pyrus communis*) – similar to apple trees, but you will need two trees grown together in order to get any fruit. Always ask about self-fertilization and cross-fertilization of the specific cultivars you're buying.

Cherries (*Prunus* species) – with sweet and sour cultivars, cherries are varied and very attractive. Different rootstocks will provide trees of different sizes; always make sure you pick single-flowered cultivars if you want fruit. Any ornamental cherry with very frilly blossom will be infertile and bear no fruit.

Plums (*Prunus* species) – closely related to cherries, plums of different kinds can fulfil different functions in growth habit (damsons, sloes and bullaces make a great suckering hedgerow, while classic plums and greengages are more suited to single specimens). The fruits from this versatile group of plants also vary in flavour, and are commonly used in gins, jams, cakes and sauces like hoisin.

Apricots (*Prunus armeniaca*) – a little more tender than a plum but worth trying if you have a sheltered spot. From the blossom to the emerging leaves, the delicious fruits (not to be overeaten as they can cause a slightly funny tummy) and the butter-yellow autumn leaves, there is nothing quite like them.

Peaches (*Prunus persica*) – best for a south-facing wall sheltered from spring rain, which can carry in the fungal spores of peach leaf curl; if you have a suitable spot, you will never get tastier peaches than the ones you grow yourself! Given enough feed, they also do really well in containers, which makes moving them away from the spring rain much easier.

Currants: white, red and black (*Ribes nigrum* and *R. rubrum*) – one of my favourite fruits to grow, mainly because you can't buy them in the shops very readily. The fruits are packed with antioxidants, and their naturally sour flavour and plentiful levels of pectin make them excellent for jams and puddings, as well as liqueurs like cassis. Prune last season's fruiting growth in the autumn, leaving the stems that have grown up over the summer, as they will bear next year's fruit.

Gooseberry (*Ribes uva-crispa*) – closely related to currants, the gooseberry is its thorny cousin, with much larger fruits that taste very similar, though slightly sweeter. Prune them carefully in autumn or winter into an open 'bowl' shape, to allow the sun to ripen the fruits and make harvesting less prickly.

Jostaberry (*Ribes* x *nidigrolaria*) – a cross between the blackcurrant and the gooseberry. It was a Victorian hybrid, designed to eliminate the thorns from a gooseberry.

Blackberry or bramble (*Rubus fruticosus*) – this is considered a weed by many gardeners, but for modern gardeners there can still be a place for this species. For those not ready to embrace the trend for rewilding to this extent, there are cultivated varieties of blackberry with less vigour and fewer thorns.

Japanese wineberry (*Rubus phoenicolasius*) – this is a striking fruit with a characteristically hairy appearance and lustrous red berries. A gently branching plant, the wineberry has a visual elegance and its fruits are delicious. They're always recommended for jam-making, but mine never make it that far. I eat them straight from the stems.

Currant (*Ribes nigrum*)

Espaliered apple (*Malus domestica*)

Apples (*Malus domestica*) – there is a huge range of apples available. They can be sweet or sour (for cooking with) and come on many different rootstocks, which determine the size of the trees. They can be grown as large specimen trees, step-overs no higher than 1m (3ft), fans or cordons against a wall, or as espaliers, which act as walls themselves.

Raspberry (*Rubus idaeus*) – raspberries are either autumn-fruiting (which are easy) or summer-fruiting (which require some extra effort). Summer raspberries fruit on last year's growth, so prune away any stems that have finished fruiting in autumn, and tie any of the current season's stems into a framework of wires to stop them flopping and snapping under the weight of fruit next year. Autumn raspberries throw up shoots from the base each spring, which fruit later that year. Simply cut all the stems down to the ground in the winter and dig out suckers that spread to unwanted areas of the garden.

Loganberry (*Rubus* x *loganobaccus*) and **Tayberry** (*Rubus* Tayberry Group) – these are both crosses of the raspberry and blackberry, but with different results. The tayberry was developed in the east of Scotland (near the river Tay) and tends to resemble the red fruits of a raspberry. The loganberry was named after the American horticulturist James Harvey Logan, and has purple fruits. Both will climb and do well when tied onto a framework.

Fig (*Ficus carica*) – these are majestic and lush trees. They can be grown up a wall but have strong roots that can cause damage to foundations, so be mindful of this and never plant them less than 1m (3ft) or more from a building. The fruit itself has a fascinating life cycle that is not for the faint-hearted.

A pregnant fig wasp enters the developing fruit with pollen on her. This fertilizes the fruit and allows it to develop. Inside the fruit, the wasp lays her eggs and then dies. So in every fertilized fig there is a dead wasp. Don't let that put you off, though – they are still delicious, and what's a little extra protein?

Grape (*Vitis species*) – a vine with a fascinating history, documented for almost as long as there have been humans. Grape skins contain a yeast that enables quick and easy fermentation and wine production dates back at least 6,000 years. Grapes can be a really useful climber where not much else will grow; the fruits grow very sweet and ripen quickly in hot, dry conditions and stony soil, so the base of a wall will do nicely. Alternatively, you can keep them small but productive with a winter prune, as happens in commercial vineyards.

Kiwi (*Actinidia deliciosa*) – a lush, tropical-looking, vigorous climber which produces its iconic hairy fruits usually only when paired with a partner plant. Some kiwi plants claim to be self-fertile but for guaranteed results, a second plant is recommended, especially if combined with a warm summer!

Honeyberry (*Lonicera caerulea*) – this delicate climbing plant is a member of the honeysuckle family, but produces long purple fruits with a delicious, sweet flavour. They can take a while to start providing fruit.

Stewed fruit for freezing

For me, this is the single most important activity of the summer for the simple reason that it means in the deepest depths of winter, I can enjoy some fresh and delicious summer fruit without too much sugar. My mother got me into stewing and freezing fruit some years ago, and her freezer is always jam-packed with an assortment of fresh summer fruits – damsons (possibly my favourite) to greengages, rhubarb, gooseberries, blackcurrants, strawberries, apples, pears, apricots, wineberries, loganberries, tayberries, jostaberries, peaches, cherries, plums, blackberries and blueberries.

Remember, this is not a jam and the sugar isn't actually preserving the fruit, the freezer is. The sugar here is just for flavour and you can opt out of the sugar entirely if you choose to. I store my fruit in recycled plastic pots with a lid from takeaways or from supermarket products – I find hummus pots perfect for one person to last a few days. Once thawed eat within a week. You will taste when the fruit starts to ferment or see mould starting to form.

fruit
a little water
sugar or honey, to taste

1. Thoroughly wash the fruit and peel and chop it if necessary. Remove any stones and maggots in the case of plums and damsons.
2. Place the fruit into a pan with a little water and put over a low heat.
3. Bring to the boil, stirring regularly, and cook until the fruit is softened and has a stew-like consistency.
4. Taste and add sugar or honey if necessary. Transfer to the pots and let cool, then store in the freezer until you need them.

Watering

It may seem like a simple concept: grow a plant, water it when it's dry and you get healthy and happy plants. In fact, there is a delicate art to watering plants well and a few key rules to follow for success. At each stage of a plant's growth, its water requirements vary and of course each has its own preferences when it comes to moisture levels, which you'll need to bear in mind.

1. Seeds need water

As most of your veg will start as seed, this is worth noting. A process called imbibition starts seed germination. Water soaks into the seed and starts to ignite the hormones and hydrate the cells within the seed which signal growth and break dormancy. The endosperm within the seed then releases the starches and energy reserves enabling growth. Once started, this process cannot be stopped. A seed drying out during this critical period will fail, so watering at this stage should be consistent. Remember that excessive water can cause rotting. The high moisture levels can ease off once the first shoots emerge from the soil.

2. Most annual veg need some watering

It keeps their cells strong and hydrated and is crucial for the all-important development of seed and fruit. A huge amount of nutrients are required to produce lush growth and fruit in a single season, and it's when a plant takes up water through osmosis that it also takes up nutrients. Without the water the nutrients are totally inaccessible and nutrient deficiencies can lead to diseases that will reduce yield. Perennial plant roots do have time to burrow their way deep into the soil, accessing ground water. This means that water and nutrients can be obtained whenever they're required. In these circumstances, interference from us 'helpful' gardeners can be a hindrance. Water at the surface can encourage perennials' roots to stay shallow, meaning they are less resilient in times of drought. So only water perennials if they're obviously struggling.

3. Water infrequently but well

A little water on a regular basis will not penetrate the soil and will encourage root growth at the surface. Whether annual or perennial, in pots or in the ground, indoors or outdoors, plants do better with a good occasional watering than with regular but insufficient watering. Make sure water gets right to the roots. You can bury an upturned bottle into the ground near a plant's roots or fit specialist pipes into the hole when planting — especially trees — to make sure water really hydrates the roots where it's needed without evaporating.

4. Mulch to retain moisture

A covering over the surface of the soil — be it gravel, compost, manure, grass clippings or comfrey clippings (these last three offering the benefit of high nutrient content) — will keep moisture in the soil by preventing evaporation.

5. Time your watering well

Very early in the morning or last thing in the evening is the best time to water. The sun is cooler and plants have more time to take up the water before it disappears. If you are an early bird, less water loss occurs if you water at first light. This is best for conserving water, too.

6. Right plant, right place

Assess your growing space to identify the dry spots and damp spots, you can plant species that are well adapted to the conditions you have and conserve your water. For example, a rain shadow beneath a wall where moisture never falls will be a dry spot, whereas beneath a dripping gutter will be a wet one. Lettuces are water-loving plants, as are wasabi, cress, celery, tomatoes, cucumbers and many more. Grains like wheat and barley, chard, beetroot, Mediterranean herbs, dill, asparagus, coriander and radish are a little more drought-tolerant, though few like it really dry.

7. Don't overwater

Overwatering is as likely to kill a plant as neglect. All plants have adaptations that allow them to cope with drought, but not many are adapted to cope when they have no air at the root so they can, in fact, drown. Excessive moisture is also a breeding ground for bacteria and fungi which can attack plants, particularly older and weaker plants or delicate seedlings.

NOTE: Remember that vegetables are made nearly entirely of water, and it is during the summer months, when water is often scarce, that the leaves, fruits and seeds are ripening and developing. This is a critical time to keep the soil moist.

Right: Broad bean (*Vicia faba*) / Far right: Perennial kale, a low-maintenance alternative to growing annual cabbage

Kimchi

Kimchi originates in Korea and combines the fermented flavour of sauerkraut with a distinctly Asian twist. A little more complicated than sauerkraut because of its more varied ingredients, it is nonetheless delicious and complex as a flavour, either on its own or with many dishes, including salads, stir-fries and wraps. Fermented food keeps a lot longer than fresh veg, and it is a way of getting some extra life out of your produce, without compromising on nutritional value.

Fermenting vegetables sit in their own juices. Make sure all of your vegetables are always submerged below the liquid to avoid a build-up of nasty, unpalatable and often dangerous moulds, and taste the concoction regularly until it ferments to a level of flavour you enjoy. This takes anywhere between two and seven days. Once it tastes good, keep it in the fridge and consume it within a few weeks.

Makes 1 large jar

1 large cabbage

2.5cm (1in) piece of root ginger, finely chopped

4–6 garlic cloves, finely chopped

1–2 chillies, finely chopped

salt

1. Set aside a large cabbage leaf and coarsely chop the rest. Put all the fresh ingredients in a large bowl with a pinch of salt.
2. Knead the ingredients with your hands until they start to release their moisture and become damp.
3. Once they are wet, force them into a sterilized jar and compress them down so that they are covered with their own liquid.
4. Cover with the spare cabbage leaf to make an airtight seal and weigh down with a clean stone. Close the lid.
5. Leave it at room temperature for 3 days, then start checking it for flavour every day. Do not leave it more than 7 days.
6. Once you're happy with the flavour, put it into the fridge to halt the fermentation process and eat within a few weeks.

Crop rotation

Rotating your crops is essential for annual vegetables, though the need to consider this is reduced if you use companion planting systems (see page 66). The idea is not to plant the same plant groups in the same beds year after year. This is because of the propensity for similar plants to deplete the same nutrients, leading to deficient soils, and for certain pests and pathogens that attack the same or similar plants to build up year on year.

Crop rotation is usually practised in a cycle of four years. For example, a root crop could be followed by a nitrogen-fixing crop, followed by a leafy veg, followed by a fruiting crop. That way, after four growing seasons, you eventually come back to a root crop, having given the soil and its microbes time to regenerate and build up reserves of the necessary nutrients. For perennial crops, this isn't a consideration. If a soil-born pathogen occurs one year, you may need to wait for anything up to 20 years before attempting to grow the same plant family again, unless you totally replace the top soil.

Feeding

It is worth remembering that growing your own fruit and veg really does require some plant food. The production of lots of leaves and juicy fruits requires energy from the plants, so a helping hand from us will improve our crops. Different nutrients play different roles in plant growth and without any or all of the following three main nutrients, our crops will not thrive and be productive:

- **Nitrogen** (N) is required for lush, leafy growth
- **Phosphates** (P) are required for root growth
- **Potassium** (K) is required for flowers and fruits

Other nutrients also play a role in keeping plants healthy, and some specific deficiencies are associated with a proneness to diseases and infections. Tomatoes, for instance, can suffer from blossom end rot (where the forming fruits turn black at the tips) and this is brought on by a boron and calcium deficiency. Stronger plants will resist disease for longer and certain plants are more susceptible than others. Cucumbers and other members of the same family can be very prone to powdery and downy mildew, which is much more likely to set in on weaker plants.

All fertilizer will contain the whole range of 17 essential elements required for plant growth in varying quantities. The type of soil you have can also affect how and how often to feed.

- **Sandy soils** have the largest soil particles, dry out quickly and retain little nutrient

content. They are handy for Mediterranean herbs and other drought-tolerant plants.
- **Silty soils** have medium-sized particles and will retain some moisture and nutrient content. They are unlikely to suffer from long periods of waterlogging. These are arguably the most versatile soils.
- **Clay soils** have the smallest particles and are prone to holding onto moisture, sometimes to the detriment of plants. However, they also have the highest levels of natural nutrients and the ability to hold onto any nutrients you add.
- **Combination soils** have any combination of the three soil types. This is what most people actually have in their gardens.

The sandier your soil, the more regularly you need to feed and water, as moisture and nutrients drain away quickly. Remember nutrients and water go hand-in-hand.

Chilli and garlic paste

This is a great recipe I was given by a friend to help deal with the glut of chillies I was experiencing one year. Freeze the paste in ice cube trays so you have it to hand. This is a brilliant, easy addition to curries and stir-fries and a single cube added to simple vegetables will really liven up the dish.

Makes 8-10 cubes

6 large chillies

8 garlic cloves, peeled

herbs and spices
  (optional)

1. Remove the stalks from the chillies, using gloves if they are very spicy.
2. Place them in a blender with the garlic and any herbs or spices you want to add.
3. Blitz to a thick paste and carefully spoon into ice cube trays, packing it down.
4. Freeze until hard then transfer the cubes to a tub or bag and return to the freezer until you need them. Be aware that the chillies have been blended with seeds and all, so they may pack a punch.

Chillies – a complete guide

Chillies are an integral part of many cuisines from Asia, the Caribbean, Africa and South America. They are really attractive and interesting plants with a hugely varied range of colours and flavours. The problem with growing your own chillies, though, is that invariably you get a glut of fruits at the same time of the year. And the more you pick them, the more fruits they produce, so you quickly find you have more than you know what to do with. Therefore, it pays to have a few solutions in your armoury so that you are ready and prepared for storing and preserving your chillies and can continue to enjoy them all year round.

Choosing

You can buy plug plants, but to get the best range, grow them from seed. There are so many to choose from and they are all ranked on something called the Scoville scale. The lower the number on the scale, the milder the chilli. And the range is huge. Some chillies rank at about 5–15 on the scale, while others, like the Carolina Reaper, are more like 2 million, with some chillies even claiming to reach the heady (and rather stupid) heights of 16 million. It's definitely a case of buyer beware, and I would go no hotter than an Orange Habanero at 150,000–300,000 on the scale. Remember, chillies are at their hottest in the pithy tissues in the centre, so if you want to temper the heat, remove the seeds.

Some of the milder chillies have an amazing flavour, so don't overlook delicate tastes in favour of reckless heat. My favourites to grow are 'Padron', a green chilli with virtually no heat but a lovely flavour, especially when charred; 'Thai Hot', a classic, small-fruiting but very beautiful chilli with a good hit of heat; and 'Aji (pronounced 'acki') Red', which has heat and produces a good-sized fruit with an undertone of lemon in its aftertaste.

Growing

Sow chilli seeds indoors early in the year in order to give them plenty of time to mature by the summer. Sow in a pot or tray of seed and cutting compost and place in a heated greenhouse or on a warm window ledge. Keep the compost well watered until germination. Once the second set of leaves has formed, prick out the seedlings into their own small pots.

Pot them up incrementally in a general-purpose, peat-free compost as the roots start to show through the holes at the base of the pot. As the year warms up, you can start to think about bringing the plants outside, but be aware that in most regions chilli plants will produce more fruit if they are kept in a greenhouse or indoors. If you are in a particularly warm region, then by all means bring them outside where they will be less prone to aphids.

Water your chillies regularly and feed them once a week with a liquid feed as soon as they start to produce flowers.

Harvesting

Once you start harvesting your chillies, they will come thick and fast, and this is where clever storage comes into play. Chillies freeze well – simply pop whole chillies into a box or bag and store in the freezer until you need them. Drying chillies is another really good way to hold on to them for the winter. Simply pin or tie them to a string and suspend them in the air until they dry out.

Chilli oil is simple to make and another way to preserve them. Wash the chillies and blanch them in a pan of water for a few minutes to sterilize and soften them. Then put them into a bottle of olive oil and leave them to infuse. After a few weeks, the oil will have quite a kick. You can also add other components to the oil, such as garlic cloves or rosemary sprigs. This is also useful for rubbing on skin as pain relief and to improve circulation.

Saving the seeds from your chillies is an easy way of getting ready for next year. You can also swap them with other people's seeds to increase genetic diversity in your vegetable patch. To save the seeds, simply remove them when you cook with the fresh chillies and dry them out by spreading them on a piece of muslin or kitchen paper. Once they are dry, put them in a paper envelope, label the envelope and store them in a cool, dry place until the time comes around to sow the next batch early next year.

Sauerkraut

This is something I was forced to eat a lot as a child with German relatives. And I can't say I was a fan. But in later life I learned that this was mainly because I was given some pretty nasty sauerkraut from a packet or tin. As an adult, I learned from my lovely friend Cornelia that this fermented cabbage dish can be delicious if it's freshly made. Later I learned how to make it myself, with the help of another friend. It's a very simple process involving only cabbage and salt. Once you've mastered the basics, you can add your own twists with things like caraway seeds, ginger, beetroot, herbs and spices. Once you've found a fermenting technique, you can then start to experiment with different veg to see what works and what doesn't.

Makes 1 large jar

1 red or white cabbage
salt

1. Discard any damaged outer leaves from the cabbage, then set aside one or two large leaves for later. Chop or grate the remaining cabbage to your preferred thickness – chunky or fine – and put it into a large bowl.
2. Sprinkle over a pinch of salt. Don't be tempted to add too much salt, as it will overpower the flavour of the cabbage.
3. Start working the salt into the cabbage with your hands. It's a kneading action, like making bread. It takes a long time but you will start to feel it get soggy.
4. Once the cabbage is wet, place it in a large sterilized jar and compress it down until it's fully submerged in its own liquid.
5. Place a clean outer leaf on top of the cabbage and weigh it down with a clean stone to keep the cabbage submerged once the lid is on.
6. Leave at room temperature for between 3 and 7 days. After day 3, taste it every day until you like its fermented flavour.
7. Once you are happy with the flavour, arrest the fermentation process by putting the jar into the fridge. If you keep the jar clean and sealed and store it in the fridge, it can last for up to 6 months.

Try adding herbs, spices and other vegetables to your sauerkraut to experiment with flavours

Courgette 'Floridor'

Courgettes – how to use a glut

Everybody loves to grow courgettes, then regrets having grown so many because there is always a point in the summer when it's all you have and you have so very many of them that the last thing you want is another courgette.

Here are a few simple ideas for dealing with a glut:

- **Courgetti spaghetti** – this phenomenon swept the world after the invention of the spiralizer, which revolutionized the humble courgette – and with good reason. Courgetti-spaghetti cooks in no time and is really, really good for you. It can also be used as a replacement for noodles.
- **Raw courgettes** – if harvested very small, courgettes make a lovely, crunchy addition to salads.
- **Stuffed courgettes** – if harvested very large, courgettes can be filled with your favourite stuffing, or try chickpeas, herbs and a squeeze of lime. Or just use lots of lovely cheeses to give a warm, rich and salty flavour.
- **Courgette soup** – rarely seen but, if done well, this can be a delicious, lightweight and really healthy soup. Don't knock it until you've tried it.
- **Stir-fried courgettes** – I used to think stir-fries always contained noodles, until I was taught a courgette-based dish by a lovely lady from Thailand. She showed me how to make a stir-fry using diced courgettes with lots of chilli, ginger and egg. It was like a Thai omelette and, testament to how simple this dish was, I have even successfully recreated it at home on many occasions.
- **Chargrilled courgettes** – as with peppers, a little charring totally changes the flavour of a courgette.
- **Tempura courgettes** – frying in tempura batter, with some delicate Asian seasoning, is a completely different take on the courgette but it works so well with the subtle flavours and has a light and healthy texture.
- **Courgette cake** – I have never tried to make a cake containing grated courgettes but have very successfully eaten one, so I can vouch for the concept!

If you've tried all of these and are still overrun, then there's only one thing for it – give them all away to friends and neighbours!

Tomatoes – a complete guide

Tomatoes are one of the best plants you can grow and I always grow loads of different kinds for one simple reason – they taste amazing. Tomatoes sum up perfectly how out of touch with seasonality we have become. We have grown used to eating them all year round, like many fruits, but when they are in season – perfectly ripe and fresh off the plant – they zing and fizz with sweetness and health. They also force the inevitably unfavourable comparison between them and their commercial counterparts, grown in hydroponic systems under artificial lights, pumped with water and chemical feed to get them to grow big and juicy (and totally devoid of flavour) all year round.

Choosing

Tomatoes come in different shapes and sizes. The largest fruits are the beefsteaks and they will usually appear on large cordon plants, which need tying up to a cane or strings in order to support the weight of those huge fruits. Many larger tomatoes are usually grown in this way, including plum tomatoes, normal round cooking or eating tomatoes, and even some cherry tomatoes. To achieve a cordon, you have to tie the plant to its support as it grows and pinch out any side shoots that form to leave just the central stem. Then you will need to remove the growing tip at the top of the plant in the summer, so that you guarantee the ripening of the existing fruits without making the plant work too hard trying to create new fruit trusses.

There are also bush tomatoes, which are allowed to grow with multiple stems and need a lot less intervention, though pinching out some of the side shoots and defoliating a little will help the plant avoid becoming congested. Finally, there are patio or pot tomatoes. These are the smallest kinds of tomato plant and have been bred for containers, hanging baskets or windowboxes. Usually producing small cherry tomatoes, packed with sweet flavour, these are very popular among those of us with a small garden.

Growing

Sow tomato seeds in the early spring or late winter, to give them a good head start for the summer. Do so indoors on a windowsill, in a warm greenhouse or in a cool greenhouse inside a propagator. Once the seedlings have germinated – it shouldn't take more than a few weeks – uncover them and let the air circulate around the seedlings, as tomatoes are prone to fungal infections. Once the second set of leaves appears, prick them out into their own little pots. Pot up incrementally as the plants grow.

Put the tomatoes outside only once all risk of frost is a distant memory. They are not hardy so will need complete protection from frost. I tend to grow mine against a warm wall for a little extra boost of warmth. However, you may prefer to grow them in a greenhouse for two reasons. First, you get extra heat early and then late in the season, and second, you will protect the plants from blight, the fungal spores of which blow in on the wind and affect potatoes and tomatoes. Blight will appear

as brown blotches on the leaves and eventually the fruits and will rapidly decimate your tomato crops. I always avoid growing tomatoes in communal growing areas like allotments for this reason – don't forget that potatoes will also host this fungus and spread it to your tomatoes.

Feeding is really important for tomatoes. The rule is that once the first truss (little cluster) of flowers starts to form, a weekly feeding regime needs to start. Special liquid tomato fertilizer works really well, but if you want to grow organically, then a seaweed feed is a good alternative. The key is remembering that you need a high level of potash for fruit development.

Water regularly. Erratic watering leads to toughening of the skins and then splitting of the fruits when they refill with water. This will mean they keep very poorly and need eating straight away. I try to water my tomatoes, especially if they are indoors or in containers, every single day. Unless it has rained.

Dealing with a glut

With regular feeding and watering, you are likely to have a glut of tomatoes. There are plenty of things you can do with them. Making tomato sauce for the freezer is a great idea. Or purée them in a blender and freeze the pulp to make sauces and casseroles later on. If you have a very hot windowsill or other very warm place, you can sun-dry your tomatoes to prolong their life. You can also preserve them in olive oil: slow-roast them in oil for 3–5 hours, adding salt, garlic and herbs if you like. Then transfer to a sterile jar, cover them in oil, put the lid on and they will keep for months in the fridge.

Tomato soup is always lovely and uses up lots of tomatoes, as do salads with mozzarella, or tomato bruschetta, which are always mainstays during the tomato season. I also like to combine them with smoked mackerel, either tossed with pasta or fresh on toast.

Towards the end of the season, you will find that not all the tomatoes ripen. This is when green tomato chutney comes into its own. Alternatively, make a green tomato and chilli jam (which can also be made with red tomatoes, or a mixture) for a spicy Asian twist.

Seed saving

Saving, drying, swapping and reusing your tomato seeds is cost-effective and environmentally friendly. It's also especially useful if you've found one you love and want to grow again.

1. Cut a very ripe tomato in half and remove the seeds in their jelly.
2. Put the seeds and jelly into a glass of cool water and leave it for four or five days. The water eventually allows the seed to separate from the jelly, which would act as an inhibitor to germination if not removed.
3. Drain through a sieve and rinse thoroughly with cold water until the seeds are clean, then place on kitchen paper until they have completely dried.
4. Store the dry seeds in a cool, dark place until you are ready to sow them in the early spring.

Mulches

A mulch is a substance simply spread over the surface of your soil. It can feed the soil while having the additional benefit of shading the soil surface, minimizing weed seed germination and keeping the soil moist by preventing evaporation. Mulches are also useful if your soil needs structural improvement by adding organic matter, if you employ no-dig methods, and if you are short on time. Many different materials can be used as a mulch.

- **Compost** – anything that has broken down into compost comes into this category. You may be buying it in as green waste or compost, or you could be making your own using garden waste. Be aware that compost can contain some weed seed, especially if you have made it yourself. You can heat the compost up to kill any seeds but this will also kill microbes and fungi, both of which can be very beneficial to the plants. Another consideration is that you must never add organic matter like this to waterlogged ground. Doing so will cause a build-up of anaerobic bacteria and can lead to soil toxicity. Add a mulch of compost to the soil in spring, about 10cm (4in) thick, spread across the whole soil surface.
- **Manure** – this has a much higher nutrient content than compost and is very good for improving soil structure. Make sure fresh manure has been seasoned for six months to a year before spreading it across the soil, otherwise it can be too strong and scorch plants. Also, the ammonia and other chemicals naturally present in manure can leach into the soil and potentially into water courses around your garden.

- **Straw, hay, grass clippings** – this is a really good vegan option and fairly cheap. Be aware of weed seeds, but a mulch of this kind, particularly the grass clippings, is high in nitrogen and will break down as it lies there, to offer a slow release of feed.
- **Biochar** – essentially charcoal that has been 'activated' with fertilizer (often urine but also things like compost tea), this is a great mulch. It is made by burning wood, so if you are having a wood fire, rather than letting it die out naturally, put the embers out with water and you will find black charcoal with some ash in the bottom of your fire pit. Bag it up and pour on some feed (urine works really well and is high in all the essential plant nutrients – think about the slurry added to field crops by farmers). This product acts as a super slow-release feed and also has the ability to capture carbon from the atmosphere and hold it in the soil. It's very good for atmospheric CO_2 levels.
- **Seaweed** – traditionally used by coastal dwellers, seaweed can be collected from where it has built up on the shoreline, and added to beds. There are a few things to consider for the wellbeing of the garden and of the coastal species. First, adding seaweed will increase salt levels in the soil – not all plants can tolerate this so be mindful of that before you add it indiscriminately. Second, always make sure you seek permission from the relevant authorities or landowners. There are restrictions on where you can collect seaweed and at what time of year, to protect the breeding and life cycles of coastal fauna. Finally, always take it from above the tideline. Seaweed can sit damp on the beach for a while, harbouring a huge range of creatures. Dried-out seaweed that's built up above the tideline should be fairly safe to collect.

Granular and slow-release fertilizers

These products offer a really effective, time-saving method of feeding, which can be targeted to specific species you know need a little extra boost – things like sweetcorn, leafy greens, tomatoes, aubergines and flowering plants.

- **Fish, blood and bone** – this is a powdered organic fertilizer. Always wear gloves when you use it, as it can burn, particularly if you have any cuts on your hands. As its name suggests, it has a rather potent aroma! I sometimes add a little to the bottom of the hole when I'm planting a hungry plant. It can help plants to put on healthy roots quickly. Do not overuse it as it is strong and a little scattering every few weeks in summer is the way to go, rather than one big dose, which can scorch and damage plants. Try to avoid getting any of the powder on foliage.
- **Chicken manure** – this organic plant food comes in pellet form and is really high in nitrogen. If you are lucky enough to have your own chickens, you can season the manure and use it, but if not, it's fairly inexpensive to buy, and a box of it goes a long way. I tend to scatter this around the soil of hungry crops once every two or three weeks in the growing season. Always follow the packet guidelines in terms of dosage, but err on the side of caution and underfeed rather than overfeed. And always follow with a really good and thorough watering.
- **Granular non-organic feeds** – I never use these because the negative impact of using strong chemicals on the environment and ecosystem is well documented. However, if you feel this is the best course of action for you, I recommend using them sparingly. They are most effective in containers, which can suffer from a lack of plant food. As with any plant food, follow the dosage instructions scrupulously because overfeeding with these strong chemicals can kill a plant fairly quickly.
- **Biochar** – see page 99.

Comfrey (*Symphytum*), which is high in nitrogen and good for making fertilizer

Liquid feeds

Liquid feeds deliver instantly accessible nutrients for very targeted feeding. They are useful for feeding pots, containers and grow bags, and for crops that produce lots of leafy growth, fruits and flowers. As you might expect, this type of feeding is a little more involved and may not be for everyone – especially if you lead a very busy life. Slow-release fertilizers will do the job just fine, so don't worry if this regular involvement feels a step too far.

Seaweed – different from a seaweed mulch, this is a liquid product bought in a bottle. It's usually organic and is really good for most veg and fruit. Dilute in water according to the instructions on the bottle and simply water the plants that need it. It works particularly well for plants like tomatoes and chillies. Start a regular feeding regime as soon as the first flowers start to show on any fruiting plant and then continue to feed once a week for the rest of the growing season.

Comfrey or nettle tea – this is easy to make by submerging comfrey or nettle foliage in water for a couple of months and stirring intermittently, preferably with a peg on your nose to prevent you from having to smell the concoction! After two months, you'll have a rich, highly nutritious plant food that can be diluted in water at a ratio of 1:10 and used to water plants. It's free, makes good use of plants that would otherwise be considered weeds, and keeps your crops looking good and performing well.

Chemical feeds – with organic options so readily available and at very similar prices, I never use chemical plant foods. But if you have a specific plant you want to feed with a specific mix of nutrients, then chemical products can be the only options available. Like other liquid feeds, they must be diluted in water according to the instructions and poured onto the soil or into the pots of the plants you want to target.

Fertilizers and the vegan diet

If you subscribe to a fully plant-based way of life, then it might be worth thinking twice about using manure. Some people believe using by-products of the meat-farming industries could compromise a vegan diet. And, of course, some organic products like fish, blood and bone are themselves made from animal products, so an awareness of this could affect your purchasing decisions.

Growing edible seed

One of the most rewarding parts of growing your own produce is when you find other hidden uses in plants you thought you knew. One of the least commonly considered characteristics of some of the plants we take for granted are the edible seeds. Sunflowers and millet are grown for their seeds alone but others are a little more subtle because the principal reason for growing is not for the seeds at all, but for the foliage or flowers.

- **Coriander** – the leaf is delicious and extremely versatile in all kinds of cooking, with a zesty freshness unlike anything else. Yet the dried seeds are very different – deep and sultry and spicy. Somewhere in the middle, though, are the green seeds, harvested once the fruit has formed but before the seeds have dried and fully matured. These green seeds have an initial burst of coriander leaf flavour, then a spicy undertone where the seed is developing. I have known people to discard the plants once they start to flower, but that is when they are about to produce their magic.
- **Fennel** – the feathery leaves of the fennel plant have a distinctly aniseed taste, whereas the seeds that are produced after the pollinator-friendly flowers have faded have a warm spicy flavour, with a more earthy feel. The aroma from the seedheads also gives off oils that fill a room with a really pleasant scent.
- **Caraway** – this plant is mainly grown for its seeds, which flavour a lot of European dishes like the *Kümmel Kohl* (caraway cabbage) I was raised on, and some amazing cabbage omelettes. Caraway is not a particularly common spice but it does pack a real punch of flavour.
- **Nigella** – this is a great companion flower for a vegetable patch, its vivid blue attracting pollinators. The romantic common name – love-in-a-mist – really does describe the fluffy, billowing habit of the nigella flowers. Just as attractive, though, are the stunning seedheads. These highly ornamental structures contain the most delicious seeds. The flavour is subtle yet distinctive. It works really well with sweet flavours, particularly citrus ones like orange.
- **Pumpkin** – another hidden seed is the humble pumpkin seed. These are not only delicious but also highly nutritious. You can eat the shell that cases the seed too. Either roast and eat the whole thing or carefully remove the woody casing and just eat the seed inside.
- **Mustard** – there are various mustards, from black mustard to white mustard. Some of these plants, like garlic mustard, are mainly grown for their edible foliage, but some also produce edible seeds, which are a really useful garnish for a range of dishes, or can be toasted as a base for spicy dishes.
- **Nettles, plantain and fat hen** – these plants are all undoubtedly considered weeds, but they have delicious and highly nourishing seeds. Nettle and plantain seeds are really useful as a grain and can be added to cereal or bread for some extra nutrition. Fat hen, a close relative of quinoa, has shiny black seeds, which are best collected (or the weed will grow everywhere). The seeds don't have a huge amount of flavour but they are very munchable and useful as an additional source of nutrition.

Fennel (*Foeniculum vulgare*) flowers, which are great for hoverflies, turning to seed, which is great for us

Pests and diseases

Often a problem on crop plants, pests can be especially ... well, pestilent, and result in decimated plants and little left for you to harvest. There is, however, a growing trend to nurture and encourage insects and invertebrates into our gardens to offer them a last safe harbour and a chance for population recovery. For this reason, I discourage using pesticides but instead recommend physical barriers to specific pests: fine mesh to protect brassicas from cabbage white butterflies, for instance, or a netted fruit cage. Both of these should have wildlife-safe netting with holes less than 5mm (¼in).

Biological controls in the form of host-specific predators are also really effective. Ground beetles, frogs, lizards and birds will naturally prey on your nasties, but you can buy in specific species like lacewings and ladybird larvae to release into the garden to deal with aphids. You can also buy nematodes, which attack a specific host such as slugs, and parasitoid wasps to deal with an outbreak of aphids or other pests.

Vigilance in a greenhouse is always recommended, and any aphids causing particular damage should be dealt with as swiftly as possible, using a cotton bud, soapy water and the physical, targeted removal of the offending species. This is preferable to a broad-stroke approach designed to annihilate one species but inadvertently destroying many. Strong plants and good airflow are the very best defence against disease.

A mullein moth caterpillar on *Verbascum* leaves; one of the benefits of not spraying pests is welcoming the more unusual species

Methods of sustainable, productive growing

- **No-dig** – the practice of not digging or double digging, nor walking on or compacting your soil, for improved soil health, soil biodiversity and soil structure.
- **Permaculture** – see page 40.
- **Biodynamics** – a really complicated but very interesting methodology that involves various weird and wonderful techniques. One of the key elements is using the phases of the moon to dictate how and when to perform your gardening tasks. The theory for this is that the gravitational pull of the moon, which affects the tides, has the same effect on the water particles found in vegetables and fruits. There are also some ritualistic practices using cow horns, designed to feed the soil microbiome.
- **Forest gardening** – this is a system that uses edible trees like fig, cherry, apple, peach and bay as the support for climbing crops like grapes, kiwi, beans, hablitzia, some squashes, cucumber and melons. Beneath this, your more usual crops can be grown on the ground, but be aware that a large tree will take an awful lot of moisture and cast a good deal of shade, which might impact negatively on nutrient-hungry crops. The idea is to recreate a forest-style community with trees, shrubs, climbers and ground-cover plants, but with edible plants at every level, from the floor to the canopy.

Foraged food

For those of us who don't have an enormous garden, or even any garden at all, there is no need to give up on freshly picked food. Foraging is a really great thing to do. It involves no growing or intervention from us at all, gets us out and about enjoying nature, and has minimal environmental impact. Be sure to follow the strict foraging code:

- never take more than ten per cent
- always leave plenty for the birds
- never pull something up by its roots
- always be mindful of your safety and the safety of others, especially on roadsides and by only taking what you absolutely know to be safe and non-toxic
- only take what you need and use what you take

You can enjoy a really varied diet and learn a lot about the natural world while foraging. I cannot recommend highly enough that you get yourself an identification book or, better still, a foraging book so that you don't make any mistakes. And I would also recommend steering well clear of mushrooms. Many are very similar and easy to confuse with other, deadly poisonous species, even if you know what you are doing. If you do pick anything and you are not sure exactly what it is, pick a little extra to take to the hospital with you if you start to feel unwell. Plants may be natural but they are certainly never to be underestimated. Make sure you never take any protected species, seek landowner permissions and only take from species that are abundant.

Nettles (*Urtica dioica*) – Nettles are easily identifiable from their stinging leaves. Harvest in early spring when they're still tender, taking the growing tips and top leaves for stews and soups. They are full of iron and flavour. Alternatively, take the seeds in the autumn as an alternative to chia or linseed to add to smoothies or bread.

Hawthorn leaves (*Crataegus monogyna*) – best picked when they're young and fresh in the spring, hawthorn leaves can be added to salads.

Rock Samphire (*Crithmum maritimum*) – is a formerly popular herb with a juicy succulence and highly aromatic flavour. Not to be confused with marsh samphire (*Salicornea europaea*) rock samphire grows on dry ground and has sprays of white flowers beloved by pollinators, particularly flies, and goes well in a stir-fry.

Below: rock samphire (*Crithmum maritimum*) / Right: elder (*Sambucus nigra*)

Plums (*Prunus* species) – wild plums like bullaces, greengages and damsons are easy to identify and delicious in cakes, jams or on their own. Always ask the landowner's permission before harvesting these.

Wild cherries (*Prunus avium, P. padus*) – not often found but a real joy if they are. They have a tartness that is hard to beat – it makes my mouth water just to think of them – but add a little sugar if necessary. Again, make sure you have sought the landowner's permission before you pick any.

Blackberries (*Rubus fruticosus*) – found in the autumn in hedgerows. They are great in jams, jellies and pies, particularly with their seasonal pairing of apple. Traditional lore says they must not be picked after the end of September.

Plantain seeds (*Plantago major, P. lanceolata*) – another alternative to chia or linseed, plantain seeds are easy to find and offer a highly nutritious food source.

Lime leaves (*Tilia cordata*) – from large lime trees, big, bright, heart-shaped lime leaves are great in salads and best harvested in the spring when they are young and tender. Later in the season the leaves are usually covered in a sticky honeydew, caused by aphids munching and excreting on the leaves. None too appetizing if you ask me.

Hazelnuts (*Corylus avellana*) – also related to cobnuts, these are delicious in autumn – if you can find any that haven't been eaten by squirrels.

Walnuts (*Juglans* species) – they are not too commonplace now, but if you know of a walnut tree near you, then gathering some of the fallen fruits in autumn is a lovely way to get a few walnuts.

Sweet chestnuts (*Castanea sativa*) – not to be confused with horse chestnuts (conkers), which are poisonous. The sweet chestnut has a much more vicious, spikier seed case designed to keep out herbivores. The nuts themselves are usually much flatter. They can be eaten raw or, as the song would have it, roasted on an open fire.

Damson and apple 'cheese'

A fruit cheese is a block of fruit that has a similar texture to a cheese. It's like a very thick jelly that can be sliced and eaten on its own or with cheeses. And it's really delicious. It is more often made with quinces, but this recipe uses apples and damsons.

Damsons are rather old-fashioned fruits, more associated with hedgerows than gardens, and have become eclipsed recently by larger, less flavoursome plums. However, in a world of foodies and farm shops, and eating local and sustainable products, I thought I should include a fairly rare delicacy that goes magnificently well on a cheeseboard.

Serves 12–14

800g (1lb 12oz) damsons
400g (14oz) apples
900g (2lb) sugar

1. Rinse the fruits, chop the apples (skin, cores and all) and place the chopped apples and washed damsons in a large pan. Just cover with water, no more.
2. Bring the mixture to the boil and simmer for 30 minutes, stirring occassionally.
3. Leave to cool, then push the mixture through a sieve to retain the purée but remove the skins, stones and pips.
4. Return the purée to the pan and add the sugar. Heat slowly, stirring, until the sugar has dissolved.
5. Turn up the heat until the purée is boiling and then simmer for at least an hour, stirring regularly, until the mixture is very thick. You'll know when the mixture has thickened enough because the surface will wrinkle when the spoon touches it.
6. At this point, turn the mixture into an oiled tin and spread out into an even layer.
7. Once cooled, turn the cheese out. It should be a solid block that can be sliced and added to both savoury and sweet dishes. To store, layer up between sheets of baking paper in an airtight container. Store in a cool, dry place for up to six months.

Seaweed – a general guide

Seaweed is a really delicious food source, free to collect for those in the know who are lucky enough to live by the coast. It is also extremely high in nutrients. The key consideration when collecting seaweed is to avoid having a detrimental effect on the marine ecosystem. Therefore, always seek permission from local authorities before collecting – certain species of seaweed may be prohibited at certain times of year.

Seaweed grows most speedily in the spring and is at its most tender then, but this is a time it's most likely to be protected because it does an amazing job of sequestering carbon in the spring, and interrupting its growth could be damaging to the environment at large. Summer is the best time to gather seaweed to reduce the negative impact on the environment. As with any foraging, take only what you need and only harvest for your own consumption.

The great news is that very few seaweeds are harmful to health and although not all are delicious, there is a good range to choose from. Make sure you wash seaweed thoroughly before eating it – although we all aim for cleaner oceans, the reality is that a lot of human waste, animal waste and industrial waste, as well as increasing levels of microplastics, do find their way into the sea where these plants grow. Always cut it and never pull it out or it will not re-grow.

Gutweed (*Ulva intestinalis*)

This is a very fine, bright green seaweed that looks a little like grass. Its habitat is varied – rock pools, shingle, sand, mud and even growing on shells and other seaweeds – and it is fairly easy to spot. It is great fried to make crispy seaweed.

Kelp (*Laminariales*)

Kelp is a large order of brown, algal seaweeds with over 30 different genera, famous for forming subaquatic kelp forests. Kelps are edible and many are huge in size, with the famous giant kelp growing up to 60m (195ft) tall and up to 60cm (2ft) per day! Giant kelp is a valuable species for absorbing CO_2 from the atmosphere. Add kelp to flavour stews and soups.

Dulse (*Palmaria palmata*)

A cabbage-like seaweed that is delicious as a replacement for traditional cabbage or, unusually, it can even be eaten raw. This is a really useful seaweed and one that has been popular in many cultures for centuries.

Irish/carrageen moss (*Chondrus crispus*)

This is actually an alga rather than a plant and is native to Europe and North America. It has a very delicate appearance and is red and very tough to the touch. Although it is technically edible, its use is generally as a thickening agent. Once heated in water, it's gelatinous and can make a really good vegan alternative to jelly.

Laver (*Porphyra* species)

This is one of the most famous edible seaweeds, mainly because of one eponymous dish: laverbread. It is often described as looking like black (although it can be dark green or even purple) bin bags scattered along the shore. It clings to structures like rocks, groins and walls and, as such, must be carefully cut off rather than pulled off whatever it is clinging to. You'll need to cook it for a while to soften it – even for some hours – or you can dry it and crack it onto other dishes. It's a really versatile crop, which, although we may not readily use it, has huge health benefits and is an untapped resource that could take a little pressure off the farming industry.

Propagating Plants

5

Mastering propagation techniques is one of the single most satisfying things a gardener can do. Not only can you fill your space with new plants for very little money, but you can be assured your plants are grown in the best way, using sustainable methods and avoiding air miles altogether.

Growing from seed

This is how nature intended most plant species to reproduce. Viable seed germinates to create offspring that can vary genetically from the parent, enabling evolution and resilience to future challenges. It's also a really good way of growing all kinds of plants in the garden, because it is cheap and usually fairly simple.

Seed collecting and swapping

If you grow a lot of plants from seed, whether they're food crops or flower crops, it really pays to save your own seeds at the end of the growing season. There is a misconception, especially with home-grown produce, that the seeds are infertile, particularly those from F1 hybrids, which are bred to guarantee certain characteristics in the offspring – either taste or appearance. This is not true. The compromise you make when you reuse your seeds from an F1 hybrid is that the plants you grow from those seeds may not look exactly like the parent plant. The colour, size or shape might vary slightly in some cases. You can buy open-pollinated seed that aren't F1 hybrids. Seed saving is really environmentally friendly, you know exactly where your seed has come from and how it's been grown, and it also saves you a lot of money in buying new seeds each year.

There are some exciting seed swaps around nowadays too, where like-minded growers can meet up and share interesting and unusual varieties of plants. It is really important that we grow varied cultivars of the same kind of plant, bring in fresh seed each year through seed swaps and exchanges, and replant cross-pollinated seeds the following year, as this is how we ensure genetic diversity in our annual plants. Allowing plants to grow and cross-pollinate year after year allows them to evolve and adapt with the climate and environment. By ensuring as much genetic diversity as possible (and this goes for every kind of plant), we increase the chances of disease resistance. Some notable diseases have devastated crops and species in the past – blight causing the Irish potato famine, ash dieback and Dutch elm disease, for example. Saving and, crucially, swapping seed means the natural ability of a plant to evolve is allowed to continue, which is one way of giving them increased resilience.

Saving your seeds

To save seed, you will need to collect them when they are fully ripened, otherwise they won't be viable. Pick them on a dry day, dry

thoroughly, store them in a paper bag and make sure they are completely free from moisture throughout their storage. Some seeds, however, need planting as soon as they are harvested before the seed dries out, as they are only viable for a very short time. These are mostly trees and plants that have adapted to moist conditions, but it is worth checking if your seeds have any special requirements.

Some seeds will need a period of cold (stratification) in order to germinate, so storage in a fridge might be the best option for these. Other seeds need to be physically damaged before germination can occur, to break down their hard seed coating, a process known as scarification. Some can be shaken, others nicked with a knife, and some respond well to being sanded a little. There are even a few seeds, mostly from warm places where forest fires occur, that need to undergo exposure to smoke or fire before germinating.

Sowing seeds

There is nothing more awe-inspiring than seeing a huge, lush, fruit-bearing plant grow, sometimes in just one season, from a tiny inconsequential seed. It's especially wonderful to see the enjoyment children get from this, and sowing seeds is great for starting fledgling gardeners on their horticultural journey. It's also fairly simple as long as you follow a few basic principles.

Water The first and most important is that seeds should never be allowed to dry out once planted (see page 83).

Compost This is also key to germination. Seeds have all the nutrients they require in their endosperm (the sac of nutrients inside the

Timing Getting the timing right is really important for sowing any seed. Some are sown in the autumn but most are sown in the spring. Late-fruiting crops that need a long time to develop are best started early – this includes aubergines, chillies and tomatoes. Other plants will do better if started once things warm up a little. Sweetcorn, for example, always performs better if it's sown a little later, once spring is in full swing. The seed packet will usually give pretty comprehensive information about how to get the best from your seeds, and if you get seeds from a seed swap, the best thing you can do is ask the people giving them or selling them to you for any tips they have learned about their plants. There's nothing better than learning from the people who have built a personal relationship with the plants they grow.

Temperature This is the final thing to consider. Many seeds are temperature-dependent. Some need a period of stratification (cold) to break their dormancy, and others need a warmer temperature before they can start growing. A warm windowsill or a greenhouse is usually perfectly sufficient for germination, but there are a few plants, mostly originating from the tropics, that will need a little extra heat. A heated greenhouse can give that but not many of us have such a thing, in which case, a propagator, plastic bag or plastic lid for your seed tray should provide the required humidity and temperature.

seed itself), so additional feed in the compost is unnecessary. What most seeds will appreciate is a very free-draining, friable, fine-grade compost rather than one containing huge twigs and leaves. Seed and cutting composts are also often sandy, which allows even the smallest and most delicate roots to force their way through. Seed and cutting composts are usually low in nutrients so seeds need potting on as soon as their true leaves (the second set to develop) are showing.

Remember that some plants will grow best if sown directly into the soil. This might be because they don't like being transplanted at the seedling stage, or because the natural conditions of the great outdoors are more suited to them. Many wildflowers and trees fall into this category, along with crops like climbing beans, peas, carrots, beetroot and parsnips. The last three need to be sown direct because of their proneness to transplant shock.

Left: Chard bolting and going to seed / Right: Egyptian walking onion, see page 71 (*Allium x proliferum*)

Gherkin pickles

I always grow gherkins because they are easy to raise from seed each year and are tastier than cucumbers. Cucumbers are wonderful plants; they grow larger than gherkins and there are plenty of cultivars for home gardeners to choose from, including many smooth-skinned types. The problem, though, is that to achieve the extra size and pride that comes with growing a decent cucumber, you compromise on flavour. A gherkin on the other hand is smaller, tougher-skinned and very often spiky, but absolutely packed with refreshing flavour. Gherkins also offer a little versatility – you can pick them when they're tiny or when they're really large. Choose any spices you like to flavour the vinegar, such as coriander seeds, yellow mustard seeds, black peppercorns, cloves, cardamom seeds, dried chilli flakes and star anise.

Makes 4 x 450g (1lb) jars

1kg (2lb 4oz) freshly harvested gherkins

coarse salt

spices of your choice (see above)

a few bay leaves

a handful of dill fronds

700ml (1¼ pints) white wine vinegar

100g (3½oz) sugar

1. Top and tail the gherkins if they are small, or slice or chop them if they are large. Place in a colander, sprinkle sparingly with a little salt and toss together, then leave overnight to dehydrate and drain.
2. Rinse thoroughly to wash off the salt, drain well and pack the dehydrated gherkins into sterilized jars.
3. Lightly toast the spices in a large dry saucepan, without letting them burn, until fragrant.
4. Add the herbs, vinegar and sugar to the pan and stir until the sugar has dissolved, then bring the mixture to a boil.
5. Pour the boiling vinegar solution over the gherkins and close the lids to seal the jars while the solution is still hot.
6. Leave for two weeks before eating so the fruits can really absorb the vinegar and spice flavours. When kept in a cool and dark place, these will last, unopened, for several months, or even up to a year.

Pricking out

Once seeds have their second set of leaves, they are ready to be pricked out. This is the process by which seeds are carefully removed from their seed trays or modules and potted either individually or in small groups into larger pots with richer, more nutritious compost.

Increasingly, research suggests that leaving seeds for too long in their seed trays can have a detrimental effect, even at that young age. Swiftly getting seeds into larger pots gives them a much-needed boost, gets them growing thicker and stronger and makes for finer specimens in the long run.

Celeriac (*Apium graveolens*) that has recently been potted on

How to prick out

1. Fill your pots with a general-purpose, peat-free compost. Plant seeedlings individually into small pots, or arrange a number of them around the edges of larger pots.
2. Make a hole in the compost with your finger or a dibber.
3. Using a dibber, pencil, plant label, knitting needle or anything strong and slender, remove the seeding from the seed tray. This is a very delicate procedure. Avoid touching the stem completely and instead hold the seedling by its leaves. The stick you are using to remove the plant goes into the soil and levers the seedling up by the root. The combination of pulling gently at the tip while levering the roots will slowly release the seedling from its tray. The idea is to keep as much of the root intact and attached to the plant as possible, without any damage at all to the stem. If the stem is damaged or bent at this stage, it is unlikely plants will survive.

4. Holding the seedling by its leaves, carefully lower the roots into the hole. Firm the compost around the roots with your fingertips, again using extreme care so that you don't bruise or crush the stems during the process.
5. Water the pots as soon as possible to allow the roots to rehydrate, make contact with their new compost and start taking up nutrients.
6. Pot on incrementally. A tiny seedling in a huge pot will take up a lot of space, cost you a lot more in wasted compost and won't necessarily be happier. Every time you see roots appear at the base of a pot, it's time to pot on into something slightly bigger.

Growing from cuttings

This process is no less incredible than rocket science. It is essentially cloning, which, far from being reserved for the scientific intelligentsia, is something we gardeners have been doing for centuries. Taking a cutting of any kind from a plant involves chopping a piece off a plant, sticking it in a pot or in the ground and watching it put on roots and grow. When any plant is grown in this way, the genetic make-up of the new plant is absolutely identical to the parent. There are several different kinds of cuttings and which to take depends in part on the species and its preferences, but also on the time of year.

- **Softwood cutting**s are taken when the stems are still green and sappy. They can grow quickly and work well with numerous species, particularly herbaceous perennials and subshrubs.
- **Heel cuttings** are taken from a small branch, including the area where that branch meets the stem. The little branch is peeled away from the main stem including a little of the join, otherwise known as the heel. The idea is that there is an extra concentration of hormones in that area of the plant and it's the hormones that govern the function of the cells. The more hormones, the more likelihood of the cells morphing from stem to root.
- **Semi-ripe cuttings** are very like softwood cuttings, but are taken later in the season when the green material has toughened up a little. This is really useful for cuttings that are prone to rot or fungal ingress, and the material is that little bit more robust.

- **Hardwood cuttings** are mainly used for trees and shrubs and are usually taken in the autumn, winter or early spring. Hardwood cuttings are hard-wearing and can usually be stuck straight into the soil outside rather than requiring expensive compost.
- **Leaf cuttings** are fairly advanced but some species, particularly tropical species or those with very large leaves, can only be taken from this form of cutting. Research for individual species will be required but the essence of this method is chopping the leaf off and firming it into compost with the cut edge in the soil until the leaf itself takes root.

Lemongrass (*Cymbopogon citratus*) cuttings in a tray of water

How to take cuttings

1. Always choose healthy, pest- and disease-free growth without any flowers for cutting material – flowering growth is generally less vigorous than non-flowering growth. Also, make sure the material you choose is typical of the plant: variegated, if it's supposed to be variegated; purple, if it's supposed to be purple; and not yellowed, if it's supposed to be green.

2. As soon as you've removed the cutting material from the plant, get it in the ground or pot, or put it into a plastic bag if you're collecting lots of material, to prevent it drying out. It's best to take cutting material early in the morning when plants are fresh and turgid.

3. Prepare pots with seed and cutting compost and moisten it in advance.

4. Create cutting material by cutting a length of stem, including at least three growth points (otherwise known as nodes or buds). These may have little growing stems, leaves or buds, or may just look like a scar that runs around the stems. These are where the hormones are in the greatest concentration and the roots and growing tips will eventually form.

5. Cut the base of the cutting, the bit that will be below the compost, just below a node, so that the node will eventually be sitting in the compost.

6. At the top, either leave the growing tip that was at the end of the stem anyway, or cut a slanted cut just above a node.

7. Remove all leaves from the cutting except the top two. If the top leaves are very large, cut them in half so that you reduce the amount of water lost through leaf transpiration.

8. You can pinch out the growing tip if you like – this will encourage your cutting to bush outwards rather than grow upwards.

9. Make a hole in the compost with a dibber or pencil to the required depth. In a small pot or cell, one hole per pot will be fine; in a larger pot you can evenly space the cuttings around the edge.

10. Dip the cut bases of the cuttings in hormone rooting powder. This stage is not always necessary, but it can help to prevent fungus rotting the cuttings.

11. Put the bottom of the cutting into the hole until it makes contact with the compost.

12. Firm down the compost around the cutting.

13. Water your cuttings well from the base by sitting the pots in a tray of water until the moisture has reached the surface of the compost. Ensure the compost around the cuttings is kept moist but never too wet.

14. Generally, keep cuttings warm but well ventilated so fungus does not build up.

15. Depending on the species, rooting can take anything from a few weeks to a few months. You will know they're ready to pot on when you see roots showing through the holes in the bottom of the pots. Be warned that when cuttings grow leaves, it does not necessarily mean there is healthy root growth. Never move cuttings on until you are sure the roots have developed well. Pot the cuttings on individually into larger pots and grow on from there.

16. Harden off cuttings raised indoors before you plant them outside by gradually getting them used to the outdoor conditions.

Alternative substrates for cuttings

I have found that if cuttings struggle to take in a pot of compost, trying different substrates can work well. Many people swear by perlite, though this has an environmental impact, as it requires harvesting rock, high temperatures to explode it, and long journeys to import it. Washed sand can be a cheaper and more sustainable growing medium if you struggle with compost, and I find water is also really effective. Simply immerse the bottoms of the cuttings in a glass of water and you can clearly see when the roots have formed. Be aware, though, that rooting cuttings in water can make weaker plants that will need a little more mollycoddling in pots until they establish.

Dividing plants

Division is usually done in spring or autumn and is used to propagate clumps of perennials, often when they have got too big. Dig up the clump and separate it into a number of pieces by finding the natural dividing points where there is a little give, then use two garden forks to prise them apart. Alternatively, use a garden spade or even a knife to cut the clump into pieces, making sure there are roots and growing tips on each section you have broken off in order for new plants to grow.

Either pot up the new clumps or plant them straight back into the border and they should grow on happily. By regularly dividing plants, you can go from having only one to having lots in just a matter of years. You must remember that, like new plants raised from cuttings, these will be clones of the parent plant and thus identical.

Scallion, or perennial spring onion, ready for division

Green considerations when propagating

Reuse and upcycle pots to avoid excessive plastic production.

- Use peat-free compost.
- Save seed to reclaim a little power from large seed corporations and reduce air miles and waste.
- Buy local seed so you know how it was grown, reduce air and sea miles and reduce the risk of importing pathogens.
- Buy organic seed to put increasing pressure on industry to be more transparent and considerate to environmental concerns.
- Use heritage seed to keep genetic diversity in your collection and avoid pathogen outbreaks in a species.

Layering

This method involves encouraging new plants to root while still attached to the mother plant. The most common way to do this is to lay a stem down on the ground and hold it there with a peg or pin. Give it a water and wait. Some plants like strawberries, figs and raspberries will do this readily, but it will not work on every species. After a few weeks or months, you should notice roots beginning to hold the stem in place all on their own. Once a nice clump of roots has formed, cut the stem away from the mother plant and dig it up. At this point you can either pot up the new plant or plant it straight into the border.

The Cut-
flower Garden

6

The reason so many of us have flowers in our homes is the way they look and often smell. A bold bunch of sunflowers introduces a punch of fizzing colour to any room, a cleverly arranged assortment of branches brings grace, and a fistful of seedheads and grass plumes gives a polished finish that can last a very long time. Add the extra layer of a sweet or spicy scent to this visual spectacle and you really can change the feel of your living space.

There are also numerous hidden benefits to experimenting with cut flowers. Putting together a bunch of flowers is the perfect way to experiment with colours and textures that you might want to try on a larger scale. Arranging a border of flowers is no mean feat and, for a beginner, it can be a very intimidating task. Just arranging a vase of flowers and foliage can give you a really good idea of how the colours and shapes of the plants you've chosen will work together in the ground. This gives you a chance to make mistakes fairly cheaply. Other benefits are a little more holistic: the sheer joy of having a pot, raised bed, garden or field full of flowers should not be underestimated.

We must also consider the vast benefit that growing flowers can bring to wildlife. Flowers and the nectar they contain are the cornerstone of the first layer of the food chain. Bringing in nectar will provide a feast for pollinating insects. This, in turn, will attract insect-eating species, like larger insects, birds, mice, amphibians and bats. That will bring in larger predators and slowly you will build up the fabric of a balanced and multilayered ecosystem.

On a wider scale, growing your own cut flowers reduces air or sea miles on bouquets, avoids collecting and harvesting from sometimes fragile habitats, and means you know how and where your cut flowers were grown.

How to start with cut flowers

In a huge space, you can create long beds with rows of flowers and many different species, laid out in rows for ease of harvesting. Alternatively, in a tiny space, you can cram in as many species as will healthily fit into pots and tubs. Anyone can grow cut flowers. Planting cut flowers in a matrix rather than regimentally, will seamlessly merge the productive areas with the rest of the garden, if there is a demarcation.

Succession

Succession planting just means that when one species starts to fade, another is just coming into its own, for as much of the year as possible. This means you will always have flowers to hand and to vase, and insects always have pollen. The key to succession is planting enough, without overcrowding your pots or borders. Plants packed too closely together have to compete with each other and become weak or die over time. Instead, choose species that will intermingle successfully. A classic example is to underpin the whole scheme with bulbs and corms – starting with early snowdrops, reticulated iris, *Scilla* and *Crocus*, followed by daffodils, tulips, *Camassia*, fritillaries, Anemones, summer snowflakes, bluebells and *Alliums*, and then moving on to the summer bulbs like *Gladioli*, lilies, pineapple lilies and foxtail lilies. The beauty of bulbs is that they can be planted in amongst the perennial and annual plants. And if you choose carefully, many bulbs and corms will come back year after year. Tulips may not, but their beauty renders them well worth the cost of new bulbs each year. After the bulbs, perennials, tender perennials and annuals come into their own. These will plug any gaps in the beds, often where the bulbs have been. One of the most widely used tender plants for cut flowers is the dahlia. This is a Mexican native and as such only tolerates the mildest of frosts; it will certainly not make it through a wet and cold winter. The best thing to do with dahlia tubers is dig them up in the autumn, dry them and store them in a cool, dimly lit and frost-free place (a shed is ideal for this), then pot them up in the spring and replant them to fill any gaps in the borders or flowerpots. Similarly, growing annuals like *Cosmos* and sweet pea from seed each year will give you a real boost of colour, often towards the end of the season. Perennials are the backbone of the cut-flower bed and naturalistic bouquets are so popular nowadays. Always choose species that will respond well to deadheading, as that's what you'll be doing throughout the season. Some plants have one flush and others repeat flower, so choose wisely.

Verbena bonariensis in among wild grasses

Scent

Something else to think about is scent. The really successful bouquet will appeal to more than one of the five senses. Think roses, lilies, aromatic daffodils, lavender, freesias and stocks. Aromas are not unique to flowers either; foliage can be just as richly scented, and also give a textural look, so should not be overlooked when designing a cut-flower bed.

Feeding

Feeding is an important thing to remember. Just as with fruits and vegetables, a plant requires quite a lot of energy in order to produce, and keep producing, flowers. Flowering is an intensive process for a plant. You can increase the chances of flowers by growing annuals, which only ever have one chance to grow – one season in which to put on leaves, stems and flowers before setting seed and giving up the ghost. They still benefit from a feed but will even flower if left neglected. A perennial, though, can live for years and years, going into hiding if it is feeling undernourished one year. For these plants, a gentle and regular feed with a compost mulch or some manure, for instance, will really help you to maximize their flowering potential. You may still get flowers if you don't feed your perennials, but they will be fewer and smaller.

Feeding is especially pertinent if you're growing flowers in containers. In a pot there are fewer resources to go round and when there's very little room for the roots to grow, those resources will eventually run out altogether. In this case, potted perennials will benefit from a regular (every few years) repotting into fresh compost, feeding with manure or pelleted manure, and a liquid feed throughout the growing season to keep them happy.

Iris sibirica, a beautiful, clump-forming iris

Choosing species for cut flowers

The main consideration with any species you are growing to use as a cut flower is longevity once cut. If the cut flowers will be dead within hours, then there really is no point in plucking them in the first place. Another crucial consideration is a plant's ability, if not need, to be deadheaded. Some plants only flower once in a season and cutting off all the flowers will leave your garden bare and your pollinators hungry. Therefore, choose repeat-flowering species, for which cutting will actually stimulate more flower growth.

Finally, consider the style you want to create. There are many styles of cut-flower displays – from minimalist to maximalist, limited colour palettes to bright and booming, delicate meadow bunches to tropical and extravagant. The only thing to consider if you're going to be growing any of the large flowers for display is that a heavy flower head, like a gerbera, zinnia, dahlia or tithonia, might be prone to drooping. You can get wires or canes to help large flower heads stay supported, but if this seems like too much effort, then stick to species with lightweight and smaller flowers.

Geum 'Lemon Drops'

Annual flowers for cutting

Amaranthus
Ammi
Borago officinalis (borage)
Calendula (pot marigold)
Centaurea cyanus (cornflower)
Cerinthe
Cleome
Cosmos
Daucus (wild carrot)
Helianthus annuus (sunflower)
Lathyrus odoratus (sweet pea)
Nicotiana
Nigella
Orlaya
Papaver (opium and field poppies)
Tagetes
Zinnia

Perennial flowers for cutting

Achillea
Alstroemeria (Peruvian lily)
Anthemis
Argyranthemum
Astrantia
Campanula
Chrysanthemum
Cirsium
Coreopsis
Delphinium
Dianthus
Echinops
Eryngium
Eupatorium
Foeniculum vulgare (fennel)
Gypsophila
Helenium
Helleborus (hellebore)
Hylotelephium spectabile (sedum)
Lathyrus (perennial sweet pea)

Lavender
Leucanthemum
Lobelia
Lychnis coronaria
Paeonia (peony)
Penstemon
Persicaria
Phlomis fruticosa (Jerusalem sage)
Phlox
Romneya (tree poppy)
Rudbeckia
Salvia
Sanguisorba
Scabious
Symphyotrichum (Aster)
Verbena

Tender flowers for cutting

Canna
Dahlia
Gerbera
Salvia ('Hot Lips', 'Amistad' for example)
Tithonia

Flowers for drying

Allium
Chamaemelum nobile (chamomile)
Eryngium
Foeniculum vulgare (fennel seedheads and flowers)
Limonium (statice)
Lunaria annua (honesty – seed heads)
Rudbeckia
Tanacetum vulgare (tansy)
Verbena
Xerochrysum bracteatum (strawflower)

Scented flowers for cutting

Freesia
Gardenia
Hyacinth
Jasminum (jasmine)
Lilium (lily)
Matthiola longipetala (night-scented stock)
Narcissus
Phlox
Roses (also good for hips)

Bulbs, corms and tubers for cutting

Allium
Anemone
Camassia
Canna
Dahlia
Fritillaria
Galanthus (snowdrop)
Gladiolus
Hyacinthoides (bluebell)
Hyacinthus (hyacinth)
Iris 'Beauty' series (Dutch iris)
Iris reticulata
Leucojum
Lilium (lily)
Muscari
Narcissus
Trillium
Tulip
Zantedeschia (calla lily)

Foliage plants for cutting

Alchemilla mollis
Amelanchier
Ammi
Anethum graveolens (dill)
Anthriscus
Apple branches
Artemisia
Cryptomeria (Japanese cedar)
Eucalyptus
Euphorbia (toxic sap)
Ferns (various)
Parsley
Philodendron (houseplant)
Physocarpus
Picea (spruce)

Grasses and seedheads for cutting

Allium
Briza
Calamagrostis
Cortaderia (pampas grass)
Deschampsia
Dipsacus (teasel)
Eragrostis
Eryngium
Hordeum
Hydrangea
Hylotelephium spectabile (sedum)
Lunaria annua (honesty)
Molinia
Nigella
Panicum
Pennisetum
Physalis (Chinese lanterns)
Rosehips
Rudbeckia
Stipa

Honey garlic (*Nectaroscordum siculum*), an ornamental garlic that makes a fantastic flower in a vase or a border

Cutting and arranging

It's crucial to remember in every stage of cutting and arranging your flowers, that when you cut a stem you mortally wound it. The idea is to choose species that have longevity once cut. The process of stem removal should not kill the plant, but the removed limb will certainly not survive. Its immediate response will be to 'bleed' from the cut point and start to seal over, protecting it from liquid loss and preserving its life. Ideally, you do not want to put your cut flower stem through too much stress. It is therefore important to gather your cut stems in a bucket of water. A woven basket may look very romantic but it will not do the stems any favours at all. Plunging the wounded ends straight into fresh water will minimize any damage. They won't bleed so much and they won't seal over, preventing water uptake.

When ready to start arranging, the first thing to do is remove the stems individually and take off any lower leaves. The leaves can clog up an arrangement, both visually and physically – with rotting green material submerged below the water giving off some interesting smells. Once the leaves are removed, plunge the stems straight back into the water.

You may be lucky and take to flower arranging like a fish to water, but if you don't, there's no harm in just having a play with textures, colours, shapes and styles. Just make sure the last thing you do before finally submerging your stem into the water (preferably infused with a little plant food or sugar to maximize the life of your flower display) is to cut the bottom of the stem again. A freshly cut stem will allow your flower to take up as much water as possible in the vase. When it comes to plant health, water is key to longevity. If the water in the vase does dry out, you may want to recut the bottoms of the stems again before topping up the water. It is worth refreshing the water every few days to prevent algal build-up and unsavoury aromas, and keep everything clean and healthy.

Oasis foam

The tradition of using oasis foam for arranging flowers has largely been replaced nowadays by a vase of water. This is just as well, as floristry foam is made predominantly from plastic, so it is not biodegradable nor is it recyclable. It is also toxic when dry, as the fine dust particles can irritate skin and lungs if breathed in.

Foraging for flowers

Foraging for foliage and flowers can be a really lovely activity, taking you through the countryside and through the seasons without the pressure or stress of having to grow your own. As with any foraging, only take a little of what you find (about ten per cent is a good guideline) and never, ever dig anything up. If you are on a public footpath or highway, then you have the right to forage; on private land, always get the landowner's permission.

Never take from rare populations, always leave plenty behind, and have an awareness that some species are protected, including lichens, fungi and mosses. Always make sure you know what you're taking.

Flower-arranging styles

Japanese flower arranging (ikebana)

A meditation method as much as a flower-arranging style, ikebana is an ancient tradition, art and spiritual practice in Japan. The aesthetic has become fashionable once again, with its

sparse, minimalist but flowing forms. Yet it is worth looking a little deeper than just the aesthetic to try to embrace the methodology and philosophy of ikebana: the contemplation of life, spirituality, humanity, our place in the world and the endless fascination of the world we can't control – nature. The form of the flower, the branch, the fruit and the wonder that each one presents to us and to the world around us is the essence of this art form. Not thoughtlessly stuffing in as many flowers as we can, but instead savouring each addition, studying it and placing it with delicacy and care. As with many things the West has 'borrowed' from Oriental traditions – fashion, gardens, ceramics and the like – Japanese flower arranging is rooted in deeply held spiritual beliefs so this is far more than just a style and should be treated respectfully.

TO ACHIEVE THE LOOK use one, two or, traditionally, three stems and no more. They can be branches or they can be flowers, but they have to harmonize utterly. One tradition uses one tall stem to represent heaven, one low stem to represent earth, and something in the middle to represent us trying to navigate our way between the two. But really it's up to you. Stop, think, consider how much (or little) you need, and contemplate the whole process mindfully, creating a calming and meditative result that can either bring balance to a room or inspire reflection in the viewer.

Left: *Orlaya grandiflora* – an elegant yet ornate annual

Wildflower bunches

Wildflowers: always the bridesmaid and never the bride, until recently that is. In recent years, the resurgence of interest in wildflowers has been palpable. Now the go-to style when it comes to planting up gardens is a combination of the prairie and the cottage-garden styles, creating a textural, riotous, seemingly chaotic but carefully constructed plantscape that combines native and non-native species. This is probably reinforced by the awareness that growing these kinds of flowers benefits so many animal and insect species too. There has been an acceptance of wildflowers – still sometimes known as 'weeds', especially by younger, newer gardeners who may not have had the diligent removal of 'weeds' drilled into them by those who taught them to garden. The upshot is that

naturalistic bunches of flowers have seen a huge growth in popularity.

TO ACHIEVE THE LOOK it's a case of playing with texture and shape as much as colour. Traditionally, pastels would reign supreme, but in this kind of maximalist scheme, throwing colours together can be a really fun exploration. You should certainly combine foliage with flowers. In this kind of bouquet it can be really effective to use a daisy-shaped flower as the focal point – it could be a bright rudbeckia or a calming scabious, but a repeated circular flower gives the eye something to latch onto in the riot of texture behind it. Branches, fruits, berries, sticks and weeds are all welcome in these kinds of bunches. Arrange some of the material and either hold in your hand or pop into a vase, adding each species and then stepping back to observe your work and find the perfect moment to stop. Then, once it's finished, recut the stems to a level base and place the bunch in its vase.

Tropical and bright

This is a much more classic look for a bouquet and what we tend to think of when we imagine a bunch of flowers bought in a florist, supermarket or (dare I say) garage forecourt. Although it is more minimalist (generally) than the naturalistic style, in terms of colour it tends to be maximalist. Bright flowers on thick stems surrounded by lush leaves is typical of this style, which often includes bulbs like lilies and tulips, or annuals like sunflowers, *Zinnias*, *Gerberas* and *Cosmos*.

You can also include flowers from your perennials – numerous iris species, *Helenium*, *Helianthus tuberosus* (Jerusalem artichoke, which will give you a crop too), or globe artichokes all work amazingly well in this bold style. Add to that a little foliage if you're pruning your, no doubt, abundant houseplant collection, and you've achieved the look without impacting on the environment much at all – especially if you grow your annuals from seed. The joy of growing tropical plants is that you know exactly where they've come from, especially when it comes to rainforest flora.

TO ACHIEVE THE LOOK think in threes or fives and keep things minimal. The eye finds odd numbers pleasing, so adding three of any species, roughly evenly distributed around the display (though not absolutely uniform to keep things dynamic) will give you a good starting point. You can always add more if you think it needs it. Huge, bright flowers can be paired to great effect with soft, fluffy textures like gypsophila or fern leaves to really bring them to the fore. The tallest flowers and stems should be at the back or centre of the display. You can wrap the whole bunch in a tropical leaf or a fern leaf for a really professional finish worthy of any birthday bouquet or Mothers' Day offering.

Foliage displays

Bouquets like this can be really calming in the home. The specific style you use can vary according to your taste and the species you choose. Try an ikebana-style arrangement of branches, or a spray effect of tiny, delicate leaves like dill, nigella or wild carrot. You could combine these with the larger, but still soft foliage of *Alchemilla mollis* or fern-like yarrow (*Achillea*). In these instances, adding a few delicate flowers can create a lovely effect too.

Alternatively, opt for lush, large, tropical foliage. This is harder to come by but can be found lying around after you've pruned some of your houseplants, or in the garden by looking for fern leaves, tropical-looking leaves such as *Fatsia japonica* and *Zantedeschia*, palm leaves such as *Yukka*, *Phormium* or *Cordyline*, or even conifer foliage like *Thujopsis dolabrata*.

TO ACHIEVE THE LOOK use single, minimalist stems or natural groupings of between three and seven stems of each species. Keep the stems hydrated in a vase, as you would with flowers.

Displays of grasses

Increasingly popular nowadays is the practice of displaying a plumage of grass seedheads around the home. Pampas grass can be grown in gardens (though it takes up a lot of space), along with many other grasses, some of which have exquisite plumage. A few choice specimens are *Pennisetum macrourum*, *P. orientale*, *P. villosum*, *Calamagrostis brachytricha*, *C. x acutiflora* 'Karl Foerster', *Panicum virgatum*, *P. v.* 'Shenandoah', *Briza media*, *Molinia caerulea* 'Transparent' and *Stipa gigantea*. Grasses can be bold and big, or delicate and ethereal.

TO ACHIEVE THE LOOK use single species as a rule. This allows them to be seen at their best. If you have a natural flair for flower arranging, you can have a play with putting different species together and allowing different textures to coexist, but this can look messy and may not have the Instagram appeal of a simple, minimalist arrangement.

TO ACHIEVE THE LOOK leave the fresh flowers in a vase until some species begin to dry, removing any plants that turn brown or look past their best and keeping the ones that have a new and different kind of beauty. Or you can intentionally dry plants before displaying them by hanging them in a cool, well-ventilated spot or placing on a drying rack until completely dry.

Flowerpot arrangements

For a display that stays alive for longer, bring potted plants indoors when they are about to come into flower, then return them to the garden once the flowers have finished. Spring and summer bulbs can be grown like this; perennials and summer bedding will also work. Remember that outdoor plants do prefer to be outside and can find an indoor environment a little stressful. In order to counterbalance this, you can add extra feed to the plant during and after its visit indoors. Don't forget either that nutrients are limited in a pot, so you may have to repot plants with fresh compost each year to make sure they are happy for as long as possible. When you bring them indoors, keep them in a spot where the temperature will be as cool as possible and fairly constant, and out of direct sunlight, which can scorch plants that are unused to extreme heat.

Dried flower displays

This can happen by accident or design! You may find that a bunch of flowers left to dry out in its vase actually takes on a whole new life. Some, but not all, species can achieve more intense colours and a wizened, wrinkled and crinkly look that has a certain charm. Other flowers are grown specifically for this. Strawflowers (*Xerochrysum bracteatum*) and statice are usually grown specifically for this purpose. Other flowers like *Rudbeckia*, *Verbena* and *Eryngium* dry beautifully in the vase.

There are also plants that can be used as fresh flowers or as dried flowers, depending on the treatment you give them. *Gypsophila*, for example, is great as a fresh flower in any display, but if you dry it before using it, it can be a backdrop for a dried flower arrangement too. Plants like chamomile, lavender, tansy, yarrow, roses and fennel all work really well as dried flowers and also have medicinal uses (see page 154).

The Apothecary Garden

Growing herbs, particularly medicinal herbs, is not exactly modern. Some of the earliest gardens documented were cultivated for just that purpose; think of Medieval, monastic gardens. However, herbs do deserve a spot in the modern garden as they are so eminently useful; for medicine in tincture, syrup, elixir (a mix of the two), vinegar, or tea form, for cosmetics in hair rinses or aromatic leaves or teas added to your bath, for skincare in balms and oils and, of course, for food. Plants can have a powerful impact on human health and should not be underestimated. Pharmaceutical products routinely contain plant derivatives or synthesized versions of plant compounds. Recently, for example, bark from the Pacific yew (*Taxus brevifolia*) was used to create the powerful chemotherapy drug Paclitaxel until the active ingredients could be reproduced in a lab. If you are ever unsure about using something, do not use it. Many medicinal herbs work through a complex cocktail of compounds, some of which can be toxic. So never dabble without expert advice. For that reason, I am going to stick to the much more lightweight aspects of herb use.

Herbs are simply the most rewarding plants to grow. If you have very little space and not a lot of experience they are easy, low-maintenance, useful and beautiful. Herbs are also useful to wildlife – for example, rosemary and lavender are evergreen and have prolific, long-lasting and nectar-filled flowers that make them incredibly beneficial.

Herbs are visually varied and there is something for any style, colour, texture and position in the garden.

Growing and using herbs

There is no one-size-fits-all method for growing herbs. The Mediterranean herbs like a free-draining and sunny position, whereas the plants that have adapted in other environments like any number of habitats. Herbs also do not always look exactly how we might imagine. From the oldest and tallest trees like yew and ginkgo, to shrubs and climbers like myrtle, roses and honeysuckle, and right down to the smallest weeds like chickweed and plantain, they come in all different shapes and sizes.

The parts that we use also vary. In some cases, we harvest the roots, in others the stems or bark, while sometimes it's the flowers and other times the seeds. A fresh herb is best but to preserve their compounds we often dry them, or extract the plant's properties in liquid (known as a maceration) in the form of an alcohol,

a syrup (with added water and sugar), an oil (left overnight for a fresh herb or for at least a month if the herb has been dried), a vinegar or a glycerite. Sometimes we use them on our skin or just to smell or soak in. Always be safe, stick to tried-and-tested methods.

Choosing herbs

Herb plants are usually fairly cheap to buy and easy to propagate from cuttings. Meaning once you have one you can create lots of new plants. Many also grow from seed – coriander, basil and parsley being some of the most commonly grown this way. I don't recommend buying culinary herbs in pots from supermarkets if you are hoping to grow them in the garden. They don't tend to do very well in the long term. Buying them from a garden centre, though, should bring about much better results. Be aware that some herbs, usually the seed-grown ones, are only annual and will need replanting after they have flowered. Some will seed themselves thereafter though. There are a few possible pitfalls when it comes to buying herbs. The first is buying the wrong species or cultivar. There are many, many plants to choose from in nurseries. If you're growing ornamental plants with flowers, yield or disease resistance in mind, often the newest, most recently developed cultivated varieties will be the best. With herbs, however, the opposite is often true. The oldest varieties or wild forms of the plants often have the highest levels of active ingredients and potent compounds. For

Siberian chive and Thai basil

successful herb growing, make sure you choose varieties that are either in their natural form or have not had their active ingredients bred out of them. If you are only planning to cook with your herbs, crush a leaf and smell them before you buy. A good smell indicates high levels of volatile oils that will translate into flavour in your food. For other uses, though, it is wise to choose the wild form of a plant or at least some old varieties. Lavender is a classic example. Some of the most highly ornate and ornamental cultivars with large flower petals often smell far less than the everyday lavender. However, some lavender cultivars do have high essential oil levels, including 'Vera' and 'Grosso'.

Growing to maximize the active ingredients

Now you've chosen your plants, it's time to think about how you can grow them to the best effect. And this is where an unexpected consideration comes into play: the stress levels of the plant. It has been observed and research supports the thory that when a plant is under stress it produces higher quantities of what are known as 'secondary metabolites', which, in some plants, can be the active ingredients that make them useful to us. So herbs will produce higher levels of their active compounds if they are in slightly worse soils, with slightly reduced water, than in perfect conditions. Although we might feel instinctively that herbs should be grouped with produce in our vegetable gardens, actually a bed that's been highly enriched with manure, compost and fertilizer might not be the ideal place if you are aiming to use the herbs in teas, tinctures or tasty treats. Instead, put them somewhere where they might need to work a little harder.

This leads on to another fairly unexplored and new area of scientific research – ideal for the very modern gardener indeed! And that is the idea that a matrix of planting – the grouping, natural competition and maybe even communication between different plants all growing together in the soil – along with all the associated microbial and mycorrhizal interactions of such a planting, can increase the levels of active ingredients in a plant. This could be part of the same process that a stress response causes, due to higher competition for light, space and nutrients within the soil. However, there are some theories that plant interactions – both with each other and with other subterranean organisms – have a much greater role in plant health than we previously imagined. It's all very new and little understood, but there is definitely some limited evidence suggesting that when plants grow in a setting that is natural to them – a meadow, a woodland or a heath, for instance, with a network of other species typically found alongside them – they will have higher levels of the ingredients required for producing ointments, medicines and flavour in our cooking.

Annual and tender herbs

Basil *(Ocimum basilicum)* – a tender perennial herb, often grown as an annual in cooler climates, basil likes moist, warm conditions. Sow indoors in spring.
— **Culinary use**: in Italian and Mediterranean cooking, particularly in pesto and salads.
— **Medicinal use**: an uplifting herb used to soothe headaches and stimulate the appetite.

Thai basil *(Ocimum basilicum 'Thai')* – a tender perennial, grown as an annual in cooler climates. Likes moist, warm conditions. Sow indoors in spring.
— **Culinary use**: it has an aniseed flavour and is used fresh in Asian cooking.

Holy basil *(Ocimum tenuiflorum)* – a tender perennial herb that likes moist, warm conditions. Sow indoors in spring.
— **Culinary use**: used fresh in Asian dishes.
— **Medicinal use**: used in traditional Indian medicine to treat a host of things, from malaria to stomach problems and bronchitis.

Pot marigold *(Calendula officinalis)* – annual or short-lived perennial. Prefers a sunny position but not fussy about soil. Sow in spring direct into the soil. Will self-seed. Great companion plant.
— **Culinary use**: use the edible petals for salads or decorating cakes.
— **Medicinal use**: used in skin-soothing, anti-microbial balms.

African or French marigold *(Tagetes erecta, T. patula)* – annual; sow in seed trays in spring. Loved by slugs and snails. *Tagetes* deter some insect pests, so make a companion plant for tomatoes, aubergines and chillies.
— **Culinary use**: use the edible flowers for cocktails, baking or salads.

Coriander *(Coriandrum sativum)* – a non-hardy annual that sometimes overwinters. Sow direct in soil from spring and then regularly through until autumn.
— **Culinary use**: great in Mexican, Asian and South American cooking. People either love or hate this herb. Use the leaves for fresh flavours or the seeds as a spice.

Tarragon, chamomile and angelica

Evening primrose *(Oenothera biennis)* – a
biennial herb with tall spikes of primrose-yellow
flowers; will self-seed. Likes a well-drained soil
in sun or partial shade.
— **Medicinal use**: used for treating symptoms
of menopause and arthritis.

Kaffir lime *(Citrus hystrix)* – non-hardy,
woody shrub grown for its foliage. Buy plants,
if you can, as they are very slow growing; can
also be grown from cuttings. Protect in winter
or keep indoors all year.
— **Culinary use**: use the leaves to flavour
Southeast Asian dishes.

Caraway *(Carum carvi)* – a hardy biennial
not fussy about its conditions. Sow in spring.
— **Culinary use**: used to flavour cakes and savoury
dishes. Popular in Eastern European cooking.
— **Medicinal use**: used to treat stomach ulcers
and indigestion.

Vietnamese coriander *(Persicaria odorata)*
– a non-hardy perennial that likes moist
conditions. Buy a plant and propagate from
cuttings in water. Protect in winter.
— **Culinary use**: tastes like fresh coriander
but gets spicier the more you chew it.

Feverfew *(Tanacetum parthenium)* – a hardy,
short-lived perennial, often grown as an annual.
Not fussy about soil type but likes full sun. Sow
seed in spring; will self-seed thereafter.
— **Medicinal use**: used to treat headaches.

Chervil *(Anthriscus cerefolium)* – a hardy
biennial not fussy about soil type. Sow in spring.
— **Culinary use**: eat the seeds and the pretty
lacy foliage for their anise flavour. One of
the ingredients of the French fines herbes.
— **Medicinal use**: used as part of a spring tonic
for thousands of years to boost health after
a long winter.

Perilla *(Perilla frutescens)* – a tender annual with
very attractive foliage; likes a moisture-retentive
but free-draining soil. Sow in spring.
— **Culinary use**: use the leaves in Asian cooking.
Used in China for steamed buns and in Korea
in salads or pickles, either fresh, blanched or
toasted for a spicy flavour.

Parsley *(Petroselinum crispum)* – a hardy
biennial. Sow in spring and allow to self-seed
for subsequent years.
— **Culinary use**: great with fish or in salsa verde.
— **Medicinal use**: chew the leaves after a meal
to aid digestion.

Lemon verbena *(Aloysia citrodora)* – a semi-hardy shrub that likes a sunny position and free-draining but moisture-retentive soil. Protect from frost.
— **Culinary use**: very good in teas.
— **Medicinal use**: said to release happy hormones (especially the scent).

Burn aloe *(Aloe vera)* – a non-hardy succulent that likes extremely well-drained soil in a sunny but not too intensely bright spot. Buy a plant and it will multiply; divide the young plants from the parent. It is considered invasive in some regions.
— **Medicinal use**: great for burns and skin complaints and can be a digestive aid if prepared correctly.

African bulbine *(Bulbine frutescens)* – a non-hardy perennial that likes free-draining soil. Protect from hard frosts and make sure it never gets cold and wet for long periods.
— **Medicinal use**: the gel is extremely good for burns if applied to the skin.

Dill *(Anethum graveolens)* – an annual or biennial that likes moist soil; may need staking. Succession-sow direct in soil from spring into summer and avoid planting too near fennel or they will hybridize.
— **Culinary use**: has an aniseed flavour. Used widely in Scandinavian and Turkish cooking. Good with salmon.

Ginger *(Zingiber officinale)* – a non-hardy perennial that likes moist and warm soil. Offer complete protection from frost. Grow from rhizomes bought at the supermarket.
— **Culinary use**: used in Asian savoury dishes and European sweet dishes.
— **Medicinal use**: great for aiding digestion.

Lemongrass *(Cymbopogon citratus)* – a non-hardy perennial grass that likes warm and moist conditions. Buy a stick in the supermarket, sit the base in water until it forms roots then pot it up. Protect in winter.
— **Culinary use**: adds aromatic flavours to Asian cooking.
— **Medicinal use**: used as a calming herb and to aid digestion.

Myrtle *(Myrtus communis)* – a semi-hardy shrub that can be killed by a harsh frost. Buy plants from a garden centre and protect in winter.
— **Culinary use**: an aromatic herb used to flavour meat and the Sardinian liqueur Mirto. The berries are used as a pepper substitute.
— **Medicinal use**: has been used for millennia to treat fevers and pain.

Left: Lemongrass, a delicious, Asian perennial, tender herb

WARNING: herbal teas can be powerful so always make sure the herbs you are using are safe for ingestion and safe for you. Always check with your doctor before you practise any herbal medicine, especially if you have an ongoing health condition or are pregnant, trying for a baby or breastfeeding.

Herbal tea

Herbal teas can be really nice hot drinks, especially if you are trying to cut down on caffeine. Add the quantity of herbs you like for the right balance of flavour, remembering that some herbs are calming and others are stimulating, some are sweet and others are sour or bitter. Use home-grown herbs, or foraged if you know what you are doing. Either dry the herbs, roots or flowers (see page 162) or use fresh.

Serves 1

Herbs of your choice: rose petals / rosemary / bergamot / chamomile flowers / raspberry leaves / lemon verbena / ginger root / turmeric root / lemon / mint / lavender / lemon balm / jasmine
boiled water

1. Place the fresh or dried herbs straight into a cup or teapot and cover with recently boiled water.
2. Leave to steep for a few minutes, depending on your preferred strength.
3. Strain or drink with the herbs still in the tea.

Fire cider vinegar

Vinegar is incredibly useful in the home. It adds flavour to dishes and makes a great addition to a salad, and can even be used as a cleaning product. But fire cider vinegar is used mainly for its health benefits. My wonderful friend India got me into fire cider vinegar and we usually make it together. She gave me my first bottle some years ago and instructed me to have a spoonful a day for my health. I don't know how it affects my health, but it certainly wakes me up and leaves me feeling invigorated.

Makes 1 large jar

40g (1½oz) fresh root ginger, grated

2 tablespoons grated fresh turmeric root

10 garlic cloves, chopped

1 onion, finely chopped

40g (1½oz) fresh horseradish, grated

½ teaspoon cayenne pepper

apple cider vinegar with the 'mother' (unfiltered), to cover

honey, to taste

1. Place all the chopped and grated ingredients in a large sterilized jar with the cayenne pepper.
2. Pour the vinegar over the top until everything is fully covered.
3. Shake it up – you should use a plastic lid in case the vinegar tarnishes a metal one. Leave for six weeks in a cool, dark place to infuse.
4. Strain through muslin and discard all the chopped and grated materials. Return the vinegar to the jar.
5. Taste the concoction and add honey incrementally until the vinegar is palatable. This should store for a long time, as vinegar is a natural preservative.

Calendula – a complete guide

Pot marigold, otherwise known as *Calendula officinalis*, is one of my absolute must-grows every year. It is one of the most cheerful plants and for this alone it is worthwhile. Calendula grows from seed fairly easily and is a fairly hardy annual. Sow it in little cells or seed trays or just drop the seeds directly onto the soil. It tends to self-seed and will pop up around your garden as long as you aren't too vigilant with the weeding. Its ease and bold orange colour are what I love about it most. It looks especially beautiful with blues and I always try to get some nigella to grow near my calendula.

As well as its visual merits, calendula is a brilliant companion plant in the vegetable garden, either distracting the slugs or bringing in the helpful insects and pollinators. Thunderbugs and many other insects are attracted to its bright flowers. I have even heard people say that planting calendula around the sides of vegetable beds will distract even the most persistent pests like pigeons and keep your crops safe.

Calendula flowers are edible. They make a colourful addition to salads or a garnish for dessert. The flavour is subtle but pleasant. But finally, and perhaps most interestingly, calendula is a very powerful antiseptic, antibacterial, antiviral and antifungal. This makes it a bit of a wonder herb for dealing with skin lesions, grazes, sore or rough skin, and mild skin infections. See page 162 for information on drying the flowers, and page 156 for how to infuse it in oil.

WARNING: Do not use calendula during pregnancy.

Perennial herbs for heavier soil

The following herbs will thrive in a normal soil, in sun or partial shade.

Fennel *(Foeniculum vulgare)* – a large herbaceous perennial with incredible flowers, beloved by hoverflies, parasitoid wasps and bees. Cut back in early spring and do not deadhead after flowering, as the seeds are delicious.

— **Culinary use**: use the aniseed-flavoured foliage in fish dishes.
— **Cosmetic use**: used to scent perfumes.
— **Medicinal use**: used for digestive complaints like colic and wind; used as a mouthwash for sore throats; combined with thyme and eucalyptus for a chest rub.

Chives *(Allium schoenoprasum)* – a delicate strappy plant with purple pompom flower heads.

— **Culinary use**: great in omelettes, salads and as a garnish for savoury dishes.

Lovage *(Levisticum officinale)* – a large, decorative herbaceous perennial; the foliage tastes like celery; seeds, roots and leaves can all be used.

— **Culinary use**: used as a celery alternative; the seeds can be added to baking, the stems can be candied and it is sometimes used to flavour alcoholic drinks.
— **Medicinal use**: used as a diuretic, to increase perspiration and to treat indigestion. It is also a relaxant for patients with painful conditions. Historically it has been used to help ease menstrual pains and as an aide in labour.

Hyssop *(Hyssopus officinalis)* – very attractive purple-flowering perennial.

— **Culinary use**: not widely used as the leaves are bitter, but it can be effective if used sparingly. It has been used to flavour alcohol.
— **Medicinal use**: used as a treatment for coughs, colds, fevers and bronchitis and externally for bruises and cuts. As with any herb, use little and cautiously. The essential oil can be toxic and is illegal in some countries.

Bergamot *(Monarda spp.)* – a hugely attractive herb with purple, pink or red flowers and a lovely scent to the foliage.

— **Culinary use**: used mainly in teas with dried or fresh foliage. The flowers are also edible.
— **Cosmetic use**: leaves used as a perfume.
— **Medicinal use**: used for mild digestive issues.

Left: Fennel (Foeniculum vulgare)

Yarrow *(Achillea millefolium)* – a delicate herbaceous perennial and wildflower, fantastic for pollinators.
— **Medicinal use**: lowers blood pressure and acts as a diuretic. Stongly anti-bacterial so chewed for toothache or used for wounds.

Lady's mantle *(Alchemilla mollis)* – a useful decorative perennial for edging flower borders.
— **Medicinal use**: used to treat female medical issues including menstruation problems and postpartum conditions.

Horseradish *(Armoracia rusticana)* – a vigorously spreading herb that can take over a border if it is happy. The fleshy roots add fire to any dish.
— **Culinary use**: grate the roots to accompany fish and meat, particularly beef dishes. Very high in vitamin C; useful in a detox.
— **Medicinal use**: acts as a nasal decongestant when sniffed, as a poultice if applied externally, or for curing toothache.

Cone flower *(Echinacea purpurea)* – a beautiful herbaceous perennial beloved by slugs, so protect the newly emerging shoots in spring.
— **Medicinal use**: used as a treatment for colds and coughs, usually in tincture form, but it can also be the active ingredient in tablets. Echinacea can be used as a cure or a preventative treatment as it boosts immunity, but it does come with a health warning. As with many natural remedies available without prescription, the effects of long–term use can be underestimated. Use for a maximum of three weeks at a time, with a break of at least a few months in between.

Rose *(Rosa spp.)* – one of the most celebrated and culturally significant garden plants. Make sure your rose is scented, high in active compounds and produces hips (of which there are differing shapes and sizes). Go to a specialist rose company to choose a suitable cultivar, or opt for an uncultivated form like *Rosa canina* or *Rosa rugosa*.
— **Cosmetic use**: used as a key component in many skincare and cosmetic products; used to scent perfumes.
— **Culinary use**: both petals and hips are edible. Used to flavour Turkish delight and rose water, and often brewed in teas, particularly those designed to calm and soothe. Soak the hips in alcohol to make drinks like rosehip vodka (see page 186), or make rosehip syrup.
— **Medicinal use**: used for its soothing qualities to treat anxiety and depression, or female problems like menstrual cramps, hormonal mood swings and menopausal symptoms. On the skin, rose has soothing, anti-inflammatory properties and is full of antioxidants, reducing signs of ageing.

Mint *(Mentha spp.)* – mints come in lots of different flavours and scents, including pineapple mint, chocolate mint, apple mint and many more, though peppermint is the most medicinal. It does have a habit of taking over the garden, so is best grown in a container.

— **Culinary use**: mint adds a sweetness to savoury dishes if used in small quantities and can be a very robust flavour if used in larger quantities. It is also used to flavour desserts and confectionery.

— **Medicinal use**: the most famous use for mint is as a disguise for bad breath. Mint can also be used to soothe digestive problems, particularly in the form of tea. It can be inhaled in a steam bath to improve the symptoms of congestion.

Honeysuckle *(Lonicera periclymenum)* – aside from being lovely to look at, highly aromatic and beneficial to myriad pollinators including moths and birds, honeysuckle has delicious nectar – just don't drink too much or there will be none left for the wildlife!

— **Medicinal use**: used in the treatment of arthritis, headaches and urinary conditions. It can also kill bacteria on the skin and prevent itching.

Infusing botanicals in oil

Lots of botanicals can be infused in oil. It is a simple way to extract the active ingredients from a plant. The oil will keep for a long while and can be used in all kinds of concoctions such as lip balms, or on its own as a skin treatment, though caution should be taken when eating infused oils as botulism can form if conditions aren't perfectly sterile. Most botanicals, whether they are flowers, roots or leaves, will need to be dried before use (see page 162), but a few, like nettles, St. John's wort, and chickweed, can be used fresh as they either don't dry very well or the active ingredients fade after time. You will need a carrier oil – olive oil or sunflower oil can work and are cheap, sustainable and often organic. Many people use grapeseed oil or sweet almond oil. Place the herbs in a sterilized bottle or jar and pour over the oil to submerge them. If the botanicals are dry, store in a cool but not cold, dark place for up to two months to infuse. If the herbs are fresh, store in a warm place overnight – above a radiator or near a fire, for example. Strain through muslin to remove the herb material, then return the oil to a sterilized jar, seal and store in a cool, dark place until you need it. Always check the scent of the oil before you use it. It can turn rancid, which you will know from its unsavoury smell. It should smell sweet and fresh.

Apple mint is great for tea, although peppermint has the most medicinal properties

Perennial herbs for Mediterranean conditions

The following herbs will thrive in Mediterranean conditions in the garden – give them a sunny situation with free-draining soil.

Chamomile *(Chamaemelum nobile)* – a low-growing or carpeting perennial with cheery little white flowers with yellow centres and an infinitely delicate leaf form. Works really well in containers or between pavers, or even as a nectar-rich lawn alternative, as it can take some trampling.

— **Culinary use**: use the dried flowers in chamomile tea, believed to be calming.

— **Cosmetic use**: found in cosmetics, skincare products and perfumes.

— **Medicinal use**: steep the dried flowers in a warm bath to soothe dry skin.

Winter savory *(Satureja montana)* – a shrubby perennial with purple flowers in summer loved by pollinators. The foliage has a peppery spiciness.

— **Culinary use**: it has a useful flavour that goes with pretty much any dish, so if you are tight on space, this is one of the most useful.

Thyme *(Thymus vulgaris)* – a compact evergreen subshrub with purple flowers. Great for the edges of containers or borders, or in windowboxes, as it never gets too tall. Can be short-lived and might need replacing after a few years.

— **Culinary use**: lemon thyme adds a lemon flavour, but the classic thyme is great for adding earthy umami flavours to cooking.

— **Medicinal use**: used for coughs and arthritis.

Sage *(Salvia officinalis)* – a handsome silver-leaved shrub, which can get quite large and lolloping, so prune regularly to keep in check. You can use sage fresh, straight from the plant, or hang it in bunches to dry. Look out for some stunning forms of sage, including pineapple sage *(Salvia elegans)* which is edible.

— **Culinary use**: great for adding an earthy, punchy flavour to savoury dishes.

— **Medicinal use**: used to aid indigestion and treat liver complaints.

Left: Chamomile *(Chamaemelum nobile)*, dry the flowers and use in medicinal tea
Right: various Mediterranean herbs in a terracotta pot display

Rosemary *(Salvia rosmarinus)* – a densely foliated, dark-leaved aromatic shrub that is covered in a proliferation of blue, purple or pink flowers (depending on the cultivar) for many months. Rosemary is great for wildlife and really useful to us.
— **Culinary use**: Adds a punch of flavour.
— **Medicinal use**: a stimulant, rosemary is used for its essential oil and can be added to baths to energize and steams to cleanse and clear nasal passages. It is considered by many as the best all rounder of a medicinal herb.

Lavender *(Lavandula* spp.*)* – immensely popular among herbalists, bakers, gardeners and bees, lavender really has it all. A short-lived subshrub, it can last for about five years if pruned back once or twice a year to keep it bushy (never cut into the wood or the plant will not recover). The flowers are at their most potent just before they open, and it is from these that most of the oil is extracted. Lavender can flower right through the summer, autumn and even into winter. Leave some flowers for the bees.
— **Culinary use**: the foliage can provide flavour in baking and in teas.
— **Medicinal use**: dry the flowers to make lavender bags to aid sleeping.

Oregano *(Origanum vulgare)* – this is a great herb for naturalizing and grows wild in many rare and beneficial environments, such as coastal grasslands. For this reason alone, it is worth nurturing. The flowers provide a lot of nectar for pollinators.
— **Culinary use**: on pizzas, pasta and other Italian dishes, it is almost unbeatable.
— **Medicinal use**: used to help heal aching muscles and cramp, and to soothe irritated skin.

French tarragon *(Artemisia dracunculus)* – one of my absolute favourite herbs to grow. It is exceptionally beautiful and hard to buy as a culinary herb. Can be tender in cold winters

— **Culinary use**: I love its flavour. It's similar to fennel but its subtle difference makes it unlike anything else. It packs a punch so don't overuse it.

Marjoram *(Origanum majorana)* – closely related to oregano but with a more complex, sweeter flavour, marjoram is a useful shrubby plant that doesn't grow too tall, offers attractive, dense foliage, gives off delightful fragrances in the garden and provides lots of nectar for pollinators. It is easy to grow.
— **Culinary use**: delicious with tomatoes, meats and beans.
— **Medicinal use**: used for coughs and colds.

Vegan lip balm

Makes 1 small tin

40ml (1½fl oz) of infused
oil (see page 156)

1 teaspoon plant-based
wax

7–10 drops of essential oil

WARNING: Because
this is oil-based, don't use
in high-UV conditions, as
it might cause sunburn.
Use at night or if you are
spending the day indoors.

Although I'm calling this a lip balm, in truth it can also be used as a soothing
balm anywhere on the body, for chapped skin, cut skin, burned skin, dry skin or
just as a moisturizer.

In this recipe, plant-based wax, often made from olive, myrtle or *Toxicodendron
vernicifluum*, acts as a thickener very like beeswax. Try to find a wax that is as local as
possible, and ethically harvested. Each batch comes out slightly differently and it's
fun to experiment with the various ingredients to see what works best for your skin.

Any infused oil will work, but I use nettle or chickweed, both infused from
fresh, not dried herbs, overnight above a warm radiator, then strained off. You could
also use chilli, comfrey or St. John's wort (*Hypericum perforatum*) which all work fresh.

Choose your favourite essential oil, or mix more than one for interesting aromatic
combinations, but remember most of the active ingredients actually come from the
infused oil.

1. Place the infused oil and wax in a bain-marie or a heatproof bowl over a small
   pan of gently simmering water and leave to melt.
2. Once melted, remove from the heat, add the essential oil and stir.
3. Pour immediately into a sterilized empty lip balm tin – you can use a pouring
   pan or a funnel – and leave the balm to set. It usually takes around 10 minutes.
4. Label the tin with the date, and exact quantities and oil combinations so you
   know what it is for and when to use it by and you can recreate it. Use within
   three months or until it smells rancid.

Non-vegan lip balm

Makes 1 small tin

40ml (1½fl oz) drops of
infused oil (see page 156)

1 teaspoon (10% of oil)
beeswax

7–10 drops of essential oil

WARNING: Because
this is oil-based, don't use
in high-UV conditions, as
it might cause sunburn.
Use at night or if you are
spending the day indoors.

This is very much like the vegan version only with the addition of beeswax, which
makes it a little thicker and silkier. The beeswax acts as a sealant to trap the oils
against the skin and aid absorption. As with the vegan version, use whatever infused
oil you like (see page 156) – dried petals like *calendula*, lavender or roses, dried leaves
like rosemary, hyssop, thyme, lemon balm, peppermint, plantain and yarrow or dried
roots like marsh mallow and burdock all work well – and pick a lovely essential oil.
The ethics of which balm to make are entirely up to you. Have fun and play with
the quantities to find your favourite formula.

1. Place the infused oil and beeswax in a bain marie or a heatproof bowl over a small
   pan of gently simmering water and leave to melt.
2. Once melted, remove from the heat and add the essential oil and stir.
3. Pour immediately into a sterilized empty lip balm tin and leave the balm to set.
4. Label the tin with the date, and exact quantities and oil combinations so you
   know what it is for and when to use it by. Use within three months.

Drying herbs, flowers and roots

Drying herbs and flowers is a really clever way of saving them, preserving all those amazing oils and compounds that give flavour and efficacy to medicinal concoctions and teas, and allowing you to have something to use from your garden all the way through the winter.

Effective drying is fairly simple and follows one basic principle: don't be greedy. Bunching too much plant material together will usually result in some or all of it going mouldy and not keeping well. Instead, what you should do is make sure there is good airflow around all of your botanicals while they dry so that no fungus is allowed to build up.

Leaves

Basil	Mint
Bergamot	Oregano
Dill	Parsley
Fennel (great as a room freshener)	Rosemary
	Sage
Hyssop	Tarragon
Lovage	Thai basil
Marjoram	Thyme

Flowers

Calendula	Lavender
Chamomile	Rose petals
Hibiscus	Tagetes

Roots

Dandelion	Madder
Ginger	(for dyeing)
Liquorice	Turmeric
Marsh mallow	Valerian

There are several different methods for drying:

— **Hanging** – gather bunches of plant material and tie a few stems together. Hang the stems in a well-ventilated spot away from direct sunlight until dry.
— **Drying rack** – you can either buy or make a drying rack for botanicals. Essentially it consists of shelves of breathable fabric (cotton, muslin, silk or mesh). I made my own with some plant canes and squares of fabric, hung together with wire. Place the drying rack in a dark, cool but well-ventilated room. Drying usually takes up to three weeks.
— **Dehydrator** – rinse the plant material and shake off excess moisture. Place the plant material in the dehydrator for 1–4 hours at 37–40°C (100–110°F) until dry.
— **Oven** – this is not quite as scientific as the dehydrator but will work if you are pushed for time. Wash and shake dry the plants, then place them on a tray in the oven on the lowest possible temperature with the door propped slightly open. Leave for 30 minutes and then check them regularly until they are visibly dehydrated. They might crisp up even more once they've cooled so be careful not to overdo it.

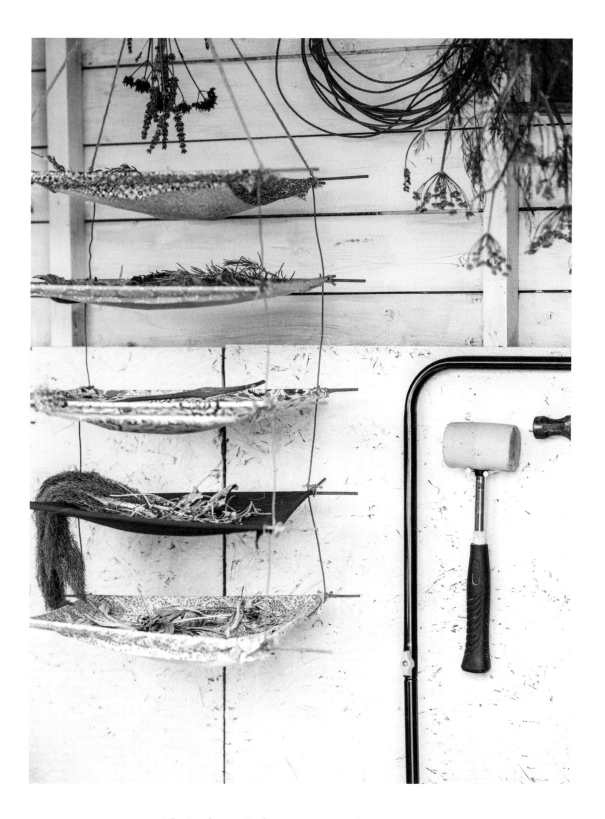

Herbs for foraging

Lemon balm (*Melissa officinalis*) – often confused with mint but with a lemon flavour, lemon balm can be thought of as a weed, as it tends to self-seed all over the place. It has a lovely scent and calming effect so should not be overlooked as a herb. Add flowering stems to a herbal bath or use the foliage fresh in a tea.

Plantain (*Plantago* spp.) – a great plant, aesthetically and for use as food or medicine. Greater plantain has rounded leaves and thin seedheads, with seeds distributed all the way up the stalk, and lesser plantain have narrower leaves and the seeds and florets are found right at the tip of the stalk. Both have edible seeds and leaves with a high nutritional value. The leaves of both can be used as a plaster and a poultice, offering a really good treatment for cuts and skin abrasions. Plantain is found growing in grassland or near hedgerows.

Stinging nettle (*Urtica dioica*) – not a plant with a good reputation due to the skin irritation it can cause, but it is a lot more value than we might first perceive. Far from being malevolent, nettles are enormously nutritious. The leaves in spring and seeds in summer provide a huge amount of dietary value: vitamins A, C, K and B alongside essential fats, iron, magnesium, sodium, potassium and calcium. The roots also provide a lot of value, though digging them up in the wild is not to be advised, as they provide a really valuable food and nesting site for many species, including some host-specific butterflies. Even their sting can reduce the effects of hayfever, rheumatism and arthritis.

Chickweed (*Stellaria media*) – delicious and juicy in a salad and also incredibly soothing to the skin, chickweed is a 'weed' with an undeserved reputation. Bizarrely, still taught on many gardening courses as one of the top ten weeds to learn to identify and destroy on sight. The simple reason why chickweed is absolutely NOT a problem weed is that it is so very easy to remove from anywhere it isn't wanted. Its roots are fine and shallow and simply pulling it gently will eradicate it permanently. Snip the foliage to eat, or infuse in oil to make soothing skincare products.

Left: Lesser plantain or ribwort (*Plantago lanceolata*) / Right: Nettle, with edible young leaves, which are great for making tea, and edible seeds

Meadowsweet (*Filipendula ulmaria*) – this graceful herbaceous perennial grows in wetland meadows, and is easily identifiable by its sprays of tiny white flowers like little waves crashing. The pleasant aroma of the foliage and flowers has seen it used traditionally as a stewing herb and to flavour wines, mead, beer and desserts. The leaves can be eaten raw and the roots are used medicinally to help acid reflux. Drink it as a herbal tea for gout, fever and rheumatism.

Growing herbs in an environmentally sustainable way

This is not only easy but recommended. Adding lots of fertilizer and water to your herbs will actually lower their levels of active ingredients. Immediately you can play your part by eliminating those processes.

Many herbs propagate really easily, so avoid buying in plants from around the world by creating your own offspring, either through cuttings or from seeds. This reduces the air miles and also, particularly in the case of Mediterranean herbs, reduces the chance of introducing damaging pathogens like *Xylella fastidiosa* to a region where there may be none.

Plant Dyes
+ Fabrics

It's a fascinating thing to delve into, exploring familiar products and where they have come from and how they have been made. With a growing spotlight on the fashion and textile industries, people are more and more interested in sustainable fashion brands and organic materials. Many people also seem increasingly excited by the idea of reusing and upcycling clothing and fabric to give garments extra life. Crafting programmes on the television have inspired many of us to get the sewing machine out and start our own little projects – whether as gifts or for our own use. I for one have found myself sewing whenever I have the time for it. And though I may not be adept and my seams may not stand up to scrutiny (just ask my sister about her now-indecent Christmas pyjamas), I find a real sense of achievement in making something useful.

I think people who enjoy gardening tend to be inclined towards crafts in general, whether it's baking, sewing, jewellery-making, pottery or woodwork. The reason I have singled out fabric and fashion is simply because there is a lot that can be explored in these areas using plants, and because we are all painfully aware of the impact our fashion choices have globally, so every little thing we can do to alleviate that problem will help, as well as give us an appreciation for the complex processes the things that we buy without a second thought have gone through. In understanding the component parts of everyday items, I never take the item for granted again.

Plant-based fabrics

Many commonplace fabrics are woven from plant material. Linen is one of the longest-standing and accepted, but fibres like hemp and bamboo are now widely used and economically significant. Cotton, of course, is one of the most ubiquitous plant-based fabrics but is associated with all kinds of controversy. The historical and present-day use of slavery to pick and grow the crop makes cotton provenance really important, as does the use of some pretty strong pesticides and chemicals, which are damaging to both the people applying them and to the ecosystem into which they are sprayed. Cotton can be grown at home but has some very particular requirements and would be needed in such large quantities that it probably isn't worth the effort. Using it for dyeing, though, provided it is recycled or from an organic and sustainable source, is a good alternative. In fact, all plant-based fabrics are good for dyeing, which I will come on to later.

I have never tried weaving and, to be honest, the very idea of it is overwhelming (probably simply because I have never tried it). However, I used to work in a lovely garden in Edinburgh called Dr Niel's, where an artist in residence did a whole project about garden-based textiles and used a lot of the plants for weaving. One particularly useful plant was the New Zealand flax (*Phormium*), with its attractive foliage in varying colours and its usefulness in a garden setting, being very resilient and growing where lots of other plants will not dare to spread their roots. The long, strappy leaves can be easily stripped back and torn off into fibres, which can then be plaited or woven to make bands or fabric. My friend Cornelia and I used to plait the fibres of New Zealand flax to make little bracelets and they were surprisingly strong and attractive.

Classic linen is an economically valuable and environmentally beneficial plant. Linseed or flax (*Linum usitatissimum*), or flax, is an annual crop that grows in the temperate regions of the world. It has blue flowers, which last just one day but in reality only for the morning. Fields of flax that start a vivid blue and fade by the afternoon are a strong memory of my own childhood. These flowers are small but very beneficial to pollinating insects. In addition, they are pretty enough to be useful as bedding in a summer flower border. The oil from the seed goes into linseed oil production, a vital component of many an industry, with uses like waterproofing, making oil paints, protecting wood and also as a highly nutritious food source full of omega-3, lignans and fibre.

There are, of course, plenty of other fibrous plants that can contribute to the manufacture of fabric, including nettles, jute, ramie, piña (made from pineapple fibre) and even bananas, as well as the previously mentioned hemp and bamboo.

Unless you are a seasoned weaver or have a real interest in learning to be so, chances are you will not be making your own fabric. I still find it a point of interest to know where fabric comes from, and which plants could be turned into fabric should we ever need to employ that skill.

The actual processes of fibre extraction involves breaking down the plant material, removing all the non-fibrous parts, and being left with just the strong, linear remnants. On a commercial scale, the process is usually chemical and known as 'retting'. But mechanical processing is still practised, with the soaking of the fibres, a breaking machine to soften them, a scotching machine to roll them, then a conditioning and frying process to get to the final product, which is a long length of strong threads. These threads then get twisted and knitted, crocheted or woven together to make fabric.

Dyeing fabrics

If this all sounds a little involved for you, as I confess it does even for me, then a much less mechanical and technical element of plant-based textiles can be found in the dyeing. As a child of the nineties, I remember tie-dyeing as a fun and ever-so-stylish way of making clothes with my friends. Generally, the dyes we used came from a packet. Nowadays, though, more and more people are experimenting with natural forms of dye that can be obtained from the plants we grow.

Some plant dyes come from very familiar plants such as damsons (a beautiful vivid purple), avocado (a stylish and subtle pink), walnut (a rich brown) and, of course, the stalwart nettle (a very pale yellow-green). Others are more unusual as plants but perhaps more impressive as pigments. These include woad (a deep blue made famous by Celtic war paint as seen in films like *Braveheart*), madder (a

deep red made from the root of the plant) and indigo (a member of the pea family that creates a navy blue used widely in traditional African and Indian dyeing techniques like printing and batik). All these dyes, and many more, can be made using plants we've grown or foraged or even using food we've bought from the supermarket.

This growing interest has resulted in some really interesting and in-depth publications in recent years. So if creating a dye garden and experimenting with different plants and techniques is something that appeals to you, as it does to me and many others, I would recommend some further reading. But just for a flavour, I will delve a little way into the world of plant dyeing, cover the basic principles and recommend some of the more interesting plants, with pointers on how to prepare them for dye-making.

Basic fabric-dyeing using a soya milk mordant

If you have never tried dyeing fabric with natural dyes before, then the chances are the word 'mordant' is a new one for you. All it really means is a preparation for your fabric that helps it soak up the dye and hold its colour. Without a mordant, the pigments will wash straight out. It does add a layer of complication and a little extra time to the dyeing process, but if you want to do lots of dyeing then you can mordant a job lot of fabric in one go and it'll be pre-prepared for your dyeing needs in the future.

Fabric choice is really important. Any fabrics that are plastic-based, like polyester, acrylic and nylon, will not take up the pigments at all. Instead choose natural fibres made from plant or animal products like wool, cotton, calico, silk, bamboo, hemp or linen.

Preparing fabric with soya milk

1. Weigh the fabric then wash it in a washing machine on a 30° or 40° Cycle. Put it on an extra rinse cycle, then squeeze out as much of the excess water as you can.
2. For every 400g (14oz) of fabric, put 1 litre (1¾ pints) of soya milk and 5 litres (9 pints) of water in a bucket.
3. Submerge the damp fabric in the bucket, mix it around and leave to soak for 12 hours.
4. Remove the fabric and squeeze out the excess milk. Spin it in the washing machine to remove excess moisture if desired, then hang up to dry. Store the soya and water mixture in a cool place.

5. Dip the dry fabric back into the soya and water solution briefly, spin again and dry again.
6. Repeat the dipping and drying again, then run your washing machine on a rinse cycle to clean it.
7. Once dry, store the fabric for at least a week before dyeing.

Making a dye

1. Put the desired plant material in a large aluminium saucepan with just enough water to cover it.
2. Heat over a very low heat to simmering point, then simmer for one hour, topping up the water if it reduces too much.
3. After an hour, check the colour of the water. You can experiment to find what works best – for example, increasing the heat may improve the colour intensity.
4. Leave the plant material in the water until the liquid has cooled, then strain the contents of the saucepan through muslin or a sieve lined with muslin. The longer the dye is in the aluminium pot, the better it will cling to the fabric, so ideally return the liquid to the pan for at least 24 hours.
5. For intensified pigment, add fresh plant material to the strained dye and repeat the process.

If you wish to store the dye, simmer it on the hob to reduce the water and store in an airtight container in the fridge for up to a few weeks. If your pan ends up getting discoloured, scour it or boil hibiscus flowers in it to remove the stains.

Using the dye

1. Slow is best. Leave the fabric in the dye for at least 24 hours for a strong colour. If you're after a paler colour, reduce the time or add a little water for a weaker solution. Tannin-rich colours may not need so long to develop. As many dye plants are toxic if ingested, you might feel more comfortable wearing gloves while working with plant material.
2. Dampen the fabric and submerge it in the dye pot, ensuring it is well covered and can move around freely in the dye.
3. Slowly heat the dye pot, stirring periodically, and simmer gently for at least one hour.
4. Leave the fabric to cool in the dye.
5. Heat again for a deeper colour – remember that the longer the fabric is in the dye, the deeper the colour will be.
6. After you have achieved the desired shade, remove the fabric from the dye pot. Gently squeeze excess dye back into the pot (in case you want to use it again) and leave the fabric to dry in the shade.
7. Once dry, store in a dark cupboard for at least a week.
8. Rinse the fabric with lukewarm water and then wash in the machine using a very gentle liquid detergent.
9. Allow to dry naturally.

A–Z of dye plants

The following plants can be grown in the garden or foraged.

1. **Acorns or oak galls** – both are rich in tannin. Soak in water to soften before making the dye. Both acorns and galls give a pale to dark brown colour.
2. **Alder cones** – rich in dye and will produce a soft brown to pale pink colour.
3. **Avocado** – you will need at least eight avocados. The stones produce a pink or pinky-orange colour, while the skins produce a slightly more orange colour.
4. **Birch** – the bark is full of pigment. Chop into small pieces and soak in water for up to a week or simmer for several hours. Gives a russet, red-orange or pink colour.
5. **Black beans** – soak the dried beans in water overnight, then heat gently and simmer for an hour. They can give light blue to delicate pink and lilac shades.
6. **Blackberries** – older, dried fruits are still good for dyeing. The strongest colour of all the berries, these produce a bright purple.
7. **Blackthorn** – produces pink and purple shades.
8. **Bracken** – chop several fronds (using gloves to avoid ticks) and simmer. Unpredictable results are produced, from pinky tans from older stems to yellowy-greens from younger ones.
9. **Comfrey** – you can use the whole stem and the leaves. Produces a delicate pale yellow colour.
10. **Common sorrel** – this is a wildflower with tall, reddish stems. The dried stems give a warm tan colour, while young green stems produce a pale yellow-green.
11. **Copper beech** – use the leaves and twigs, simmering gently to create putty-pink colours.
12. **Coreopsis** – collect the flowers and allow to dry a little before use. They give a rich ochre or burnt orange colour.

13. **Elderberry** – purple or lilac dyes are possible from the berries.
14. **Eucalyptus** – needs at least two hours of simmering to create many different shades, depending on the variety of tree. Colours vary from dark tan to dark orange.
15. **Hawthorn** – the flowers give delicate yellow-green tones if you simmer gently. Branches and berries give pinks. The dye water turns from green to pink over a 24-hour period.
16. **Indigo** – a non-hardy annual member of the pea family. The method to obtain an intense navy colour is complicated, but to achieve a lovely shade of soft blue, crush the fresh leaves with some salt in an aluminium bowl.
17. **Madder** – only the roots of this plant produce dye, so growing it is a long-term investment. Harvest the roots after two years of growth to obtain a lovely red, pink or maroon colour. You can add chalk to the liquid to get a bright red colour.
18. **Nettle** – early picking produces pale green and yellow tones, and later harvesting will produce khaki and warm tans.
19. **Onion skins** – red onion skins give a strong red-brown to khaki colour, while the skins of yellow onions give ochre shades. You will need lots of skins to get a good colour.
20. **Red cabbage** – gently simmer and use the dye immediately to avoid cabbage smells. It produces a cool blue to pale purple colour.
21. **Rhubarb leaves** – these produce butter-yellow to pale ochre. Make the dye in a well-ventilated space, as it is poisonous and produces oxalic acid. The roots can be used to create an ochre colour.
22. **Rosehips** – you will need lots of hips to make a dye. Crush and boil the hips to create a nude pink colour. Protect your skin from the itching hairs found within the hips.
23. **Rowan** – lots of berries are needed for this dye. Crush and simmer berries for an hour.

Leave the fabric in the dye for a long time, as the colour is a pale, delicate pink.

24. *Rudbeckia hirta* (black-eyed Susan) – harvest the flowers as they begin to wilt. Collect and dry them until you have enough. Simmer gently for an hour. Produces a putty-brown colour.
25. **Walnut** – wear gloves so that you don't stain your hands. Shell the nuts and use the husks to make a very rich dye giving a pale brown colour.
26. **Weld/dyer's weed** – all parts of the plant can be used to produce a bright yellow colour. In the plant's first year, pick the longest leaves.
27. **Willow** – both leaves and bark produce dye. Use twigs and leaves chopped roughly. Simmer for a long time. The dye will look yellow at first but after a couple of days it turns a deep russet or orange-pink.
28. **Woad** – this famous dye plant can be grown fairly easily in temperate gardens, but the dye process is fairly involved and requires high-tech methods, so you will need to do some specialist research.

Left: Avocado skins and stones to create a beautiful pink / Right: Coreopsis (*Coreopsis verticillata*)

Drinks

9

With the exception of mead, which is made from honey, plant materials form the basis for pretty much all alcohol, the world over. Rum is made from sugar cane, vodka from potatoes, wine from grapes, sake from rice and whisky from barley. Alcohol is created by the fermentation of natural products. Yeast (a fungus) feeds on sugars, naturally found in many plant products and structures, to begin the process of fermentation, which results in intoxicating alcohol.

Beer is made from barley and flavoured with hops, while gin is made from grain and flavoured with juniper. In fact, the infusion of other botanicals to flavour alcoholic drinks has a long, rich and fascinating history, with medicinal tinctures, religious ceremonies, overindulgence, alcohol bans and smuggling along the way. Booze has been infused by monks, wise men and women (and not-so-wise men and women) for many a century.

This chapter offers some recipes for a few homemade tipples flavoured with plants and produce from the garden or hedgerow. And for those who actually prefer not to drink booze, there are some lovely recipes that can be used as a mixer for a cocktail, or can simply be diluted in water for a refreshing summer drink. For those who prefer just the drinking and not the making, try freezing a little edible flower such as borage, viola, calendula, day lily or nasturtium in an ice cube to add a touch of something colourful and personal to your daiquiri or designer G&T.

Elderflower cordial

I love elder. It is a beautiful shrub, a valuable part of the hedgerow, and a thoroughly useful plant – with edible flowers and fruits and plenty left for the bees and birds. Elderflower cordial is a drink that I absolutely relish on a hot, sunny day. It does contain some sugar in order to preserve it successfully, but you can reduce the quantities for a sharper flavour, which I love.

Make sure you have accurately identified the flowers. Elders are medium to large shrubs, with flat inflorescences covered in lots of little cream flowers. They flower at the same time as other plants with similar flowers, like guelder rose, angelica, hogweed and, crucially, hemlock, which is a poisonous herbaceous perennial and can grow in similar areas. Elderflowers have a distinct uric acid smell and the plants are definitely shrubs. Correct plant identification is vital when foraging anything from the wild.

Pick elderflowers when they are first in flower, in the early summer. They will be packed with flavour then. If the flowers are too mature, they may have lost some of that flavour. As with any foraging, be mindful of your impact. It is never considerate to overharvest. If foraging seems a step too far for you, grow elder in your garden – in fact some of the purple forms with pink flowers make a gorgeous pink version of the cordial!

Makes 1 litre (1¾ pints)

20 elderflower heads, freshly opened

1½ lemons, peeled and chopped

1½ litres (2¾ pints) boiling water

750g (1lb 10oz) sugar

1–5 teaspoons citric acid, to taste

1. Place the elderflowers and lemon in a large bowl and pour over the boiling water. Cover and leave at room temperature overnight or in the fridge for a few days.
2. Strain through muslin into a large pan and discard the lemon and flowers.
3. Add the sugar and slowly bring to the boil, stirring until the sugar dissolves.
4. Taste the liquid and add citric acid until you are happy with the flavour. I like it quite sour.
5. Pour the liquid into sterilized bottles and store in a cool, dark place. It can keep for months or even a year or two but look out for mould if you've had it for some time. If you spot mould, don't drink it.

Hops and why everyone should grow them

I grew up in what used to be the hop-growing capital of the UK: Kent. Now Herefordshire has taken over in the UK, and hops are grown in many places around the world – the hops of eastern Europe are world famous, and there is a trend for 'New World' hops from the USA and New Zealand, with more robust, citrussy and bitter flavours creating the craft beers we have all come to know. I have never personally brewed with them but I am part of a cooperative, or community farm, in which people grow the hops in their gardens or allotments, and then harvest them all together to pool the collection, send it off to a local brewery and get heavily discounted beer. It's a really great system and you get to meet lots of lovely folk.

Aside from their traditional use in beer manufacture, hops are also a delicious vegetable. The hop is actually an herbaceous perennial that dies back to the ground each autumn and reshoots each spring. The newly emerging shoots can be cut off and cooked just like asparagus.

As a climber, the plant is prolific, putting on a huge amount of growth in just one season. It is really useful for hiding unsightly features like compost bins or the neighbour's garden. Just supply it with a nice deep hole (the roots grow deep), a rich soil and some baling twine to wind its way around as it climbs.

But perhaps the most compelling reason to choose hops is their huge benefit to species of butterfly. Around the world, around 135 different species of butterfly and moth use hops to lay their eggs. Butterflies and moths are struggling at the moment and need all the help they can get from our gardens.

Above: A hop (*Humulus lupulus* 'Prima Donna') climbing some baling twine / Right: Love-in-a-mist (*Nigella*), after flowering beautiful and delicious seeds it makes a great addition to dishes, sweet or savoury

Sloe or damson gin

I can't possibly overlook this classic. In the 1990s, my parents – overgrown hippies who misspent their youth in the 1960s – would drag me and my two sisters along the cold, autumn hedgerows after a frost (because that's when you need to pick sloes) to gather as many fruits as we could to make flagon after flagon of sloe gin. My parents separated shortly afterwards (probably unrelated) and the sloe gin went mostly undrunk ... until my sisters and I grew up and discovered the flagons in the back of a shed. Now we usually spend Christmas drinking fortified sloe gin that's turned syrupy in its dotage. Sometimes, in fact, it needs diluting with ... wait for it ... more gin.

Damsons are at their prime just a touch earlier than sloes – look from mid-August until October, when the sun is still warm. Other than timing, they are sometimes hard to distinguish from sloes and, indeed, the two plants will often hybridize in the wild. The flavour, though, is completely different. If you are using damsons, reduce the sugar a little.

Makes 1.25 litres (2 pints)

500g (1lb 2oz) sloes
  or damsons
1 litre (1¾ pints) gin
250g (9oz) caster sugar

1. Pick the sloes after a frost, if possible, or put them in the freezer to rupture the skins. Rinse the fruits thoroughly.
2. Place the fruit into a large jar or bottle and add the gin and sugar.
3. Leave at room temperature, shaking the jar well once a day for a week or two until the sugar has dissolved.
4. Leave in a cool, dark place for as long as you can, but at least three months.
5. Pass through muslin into sterilized bottles. The gin will last for years if kept in a cool and dark place. Enjoy!

Ginger tea

Known to aid digestion and be a really rewarding plant, ginger takes a while to break its dormancy but then grows really vigorously. You can buy ginger roots fairly cheaply in the shops and you should be able to grow a plant from them, so long as they are firm and healthy. Place the roots (or rhizomes) horizontally just beneath the surface of the soil and keep them warm and fairly well watered in the spring until they start to shoot.

Once they grow, they do so quickly and after a year you can divide the plant and start harvesting the roots. From then on it will produce roots at a rate of knots. Remember it does die back in the winter and take a long time coming up again in the spring, so don't panic, you probably haven't killed it.

Ginger is great in hot and cold drinks and has a soothing effect on the stomach and a pleasant burning sensation on a sore throat.

Serves 1

a small chunk of
    root ginger

1 mint sprig (optional)

1 teaspoon honey
    (optional)

boiling water

1. Slice the ginger root into fine discs – you don't have to remove the skin. Place in a mug with the mint and honey, if using.
2. Pour on boiling water and leave it to steep for a few minutes before drinking. You can put this on the hob and heat for a stronger flavour. Drink once the water is cool enough.
3. Reuse the ginger for a second, slightly weaker, cup.

Rosehip vodka

Rosehips can be found in hedgerows and gardens in most temperate regions. They come in different colours, shapes and sizes, and not all roses produce rosehips, but the dog rose (*Rosa canina*) with its oval, firm fruits is probably best for flavouring vodka. An alternative is *Rosa rugosa*, but the hips are a little softer and it's more likely to be a messy job. If you're feeling adventurous, replace the rosehips with hawthorn berries, rowan berries or a mixture of them all.

Makes 1.2 litres (2 pints)

500g (1lb 2oz) rosehips

200g (7oz) caster sugar

1 litre (1¾ pints) vodka

1. Clean the rosehips and place in a large airtight jar with the sugar. For best results, chop or prick the rosehips first.
2. Pour over the vodka and shake well.
3. Store in a cool, dark place, shaking the jar each week.
4. After at least four months, strain through muslin into a sterilized jar and discard the rosehips.
5. Store for as long as you can before drinking to allow the mixture to mature.

Blackcurrant vodka

I REALLY love blackcurrants. Picking them without bruising them can be a little tricky, though, and if you bruise the fruit, it will need eating immediately. Usually this is no problem at all for me, but on the odd occasion when I have eaten enough blackcurrants, I make a vodka-based liqueur. You could use rum, brandy or gin, but vodka has the most neutral taste, so I like that best. You could also use gooseberries, rosehips, rowan berries, raspberries or blackberries, but blackcurrants have a really rich flavour.

Makes 1.2 litres (2 pints)

700g (1lb 9oz)
   blackcurrants
1 litre (1¾ pints) vodka
200g (7oz) caster sugar

1. Place the fruit in a large jar or bottle and add the vodka and sugar.
2. Leave at room temperature, shaking the jar well once a day for a week or two until the sugar has dissolved.
3. Leave in a cool, dark place for as long as you can, but at least three months.
4. Pass through muslin into sterilized bottles, trying not to squish the currants, as the pulp that enters the liquid will reduce its shelf life. Blackcurrant vodka will last for years if kept in a cool and dark place.

Index

Clary sage (*Salvia sclarea*)

An Hachette UK Company
www.hachette.co.uk

First published in Great Britain in 2022 by
Kyle Books, an imprint of Octopus Publishing Group Limited
Carmelite House
50 Victoria Embankment
London EC4Y 0DZ
www.kylebooks.co.uk

ISBN: 978 0 85783 943 5

Text copyright © Frances Tophill 2022
Design and layout copyright © Octopus Publishing Group
Ltd 2022
Photography copyright © Rachel Warne 2022

Distributed in the US by Hachette Book Group, 1290 Avenue
of the Americas, 4th and 5th Floors, New York, NY 10104

Distributed in Canada by Canadian Manda Group, 664
Annette St., Toronto, Ontario, Canada M6S 2C8

Frances Tophill is hereby identified as the author of this
work in accordance with Section 77 of the Copyright,
Designs and Patents Act 1988

Publisher: Jo Copestick
Publishing Director: Judith Hannam
Senior Commissioning Editor: Louise McKeever
Design: Studio Polka
Photography: Rachel Warne
Production: Caroline Alberti

A Cataloguing in Publication record for this title is available
from the British Library

Printed and bound in China
10 9 8 7 6 5 4 3 2 1

Acknowledgements

In writing a book, and making a gardener, there are so many people to thank along the way. But before that, I would like to thank the plants that have taught me, the ground that has nourished me, the rain, the wind and all the mysteries of the natural world. I sometimes take it for granted and forget to remember how lucky I am. So, I take this opportunity to say thank you.

For opening my eyes to wild plant wisdom, Melissa Harvey at *Wyseworts*, India Hunt at *Earth Song Herbal*, Ruth Stout – though I sadly never met her, my grandma and my mother. A special mention also to Cornelia Altgård, the image of you making hawthorn vodka, rowan vodka, sauerkraut and a vinegar, all before 7am, when you were supposed to be ill will always make me smile. Thank you to Mandy Barber at Incredible Vegetables, for sharing your perennial crops and letting us photograph your beautiful field. Thanks too to the Harris Bugg Studio (*www.harrisbug.com*) for the beautiful location. Your superb planting schemes have elevated this book and I am so grateful for your kindness. Thank you to Sarah and Robbie Richardson at Greatcombe in Holne (*www.ngs.org*), for lending us your stunning garden – and my snail! Jeanette Tucker at Sage Green Growing, you are an inspiration, a force of nature and a wonderful grower. Thank you for everything and especially for letting me cook in your walled garden! Thank you to my great friend Jasmin Douglas and her mum, Nadia, for letting us photograph their amazing kitchen garden. To Mum, Dad, Bid, Charlie, Horatio, Sacha and Steve, as ever for your love and support, and often a roof over my head. I must also thank Ian, Steve, Kelvin and everyone at Worth Allotments for putting up with photography and the like, and mostly, for putting up with my weeds.

This was made possible by a wonderful group of people, whose knowledge and patience have made this into a real-life book. I am so grateful to my editor, Louise McKeever. You have always been positive and encouraging and done everything with a smile. Thank you. Rachel Warne, once again your magnificent photography has brought these words to life with a beauty I could not have imagined. Lucy Sykes-Thompson for your amazing design, refined eye and your patience. Thanks too to Joanna Smith for keeping my writing on track and for everyone at Kyle books, but in particular Judith Hannam and Joanna Copestick. To Charlotte Robertson, my literary agent, and Fiona Kimbell, my agent, you are both ever-supportive and kind and always there when I need advice, and for that I truly thank you.